Jim Blankenship, CFP®, EA

A
Social Security
Owner's Manual

YOUR GUIDE TO
SOCIAL SECURITY
RETIREMENT, DEPENDENT'S
AND SURVIVOR'S BENEFITS

About the author

Jim Blankenship is a financial planner based in New Berlin, Illinois. Through his Fee-Only financial planning practice, Jim provides unbiased financial advice to individuals from all walks of life.

Jim Blankenship, CFP® , EA
Jim@BlankenshipFinancial.com

★LINKS

Book: http://SocialSecurityOwnersManual.com
Website: http://www.BlankenshipFinancial.com
Blog: http://financialducksinarow.com

Dedication

This book is dedicated to my wife Nancy, the love of my life, my best friend, and my greatest supporter.

Acknowledgements

I want to acknowledge the efforts of my colleagues who graciously invested their time and talents into the review, editing, and fact-checking of this book:

Roger Streit, Andy Tilp, Michael Timmerman, Andy Claybrook, Tom Nowak, Robert Schmansky, John Vyge, Buz Livingston, Michael Terry, Mark Gibbs, Charles Buck, Robert Stanley, Steve Ellisor, Shawn Koch, David Barnett, Cynthia Petzold, Donald Webb, Joe Goodman, Lea Ann Knight, Kathleen Campbell, Josh Giminez, Diane Blackwelder, Thomas Horton, Laura Scharr-Bykowsky, Jean Keener, and Steven Young.

Your efforts and recommendations improved the book immeasurably – I am deeply indebted to each of you, thanks a million!

Table of contents

Table of tables

Forward

Type the word "retirement" into your favorite web browser and you'll easily tap into over 200,000 webpages. And the top two, non-advertised sites, are for the Social Security Administration. That seems appropriate considering the importance of Social Security to the success of our retirement plans. You can get all of the information you should ever need to know about retirement in just 0.02 seconds. Or maybe not...

We live in an age of nearly instant access to information. This information may be from great articles or mind expanding academic research, or simply the opinions of anonymous individuals who feel entitled to respond authoritatively to others' research and publications.

More information doesn't necessarily translate into better financial decision making. The overload is actually counterproductive. Whether the subject is determining if you can afford to retire, or how best to fund your retirement income needs, you'll find the complete spectrum of opinions on the web. I didn't say digesting this information and turning it into usable knowledge for your situation was going to be easy. It's just readily available.

On the web or in a printed publication, it's not necessarily inappropriate to have different viewpoints on a subject involving personal finance. However, personal financial planning is something altogether different. It's very personal and it's all about planning. The finance part is the only overlapping component. Of course there are concrete rules that apply to certain subjects, like taxes and eligibility requirements. But, the most important issues have to do with your personal circumstances, and how you and your family would best be served under various strategies or approaches. This is the essence of personal financial planning... knowing how to apply information in the most appropriate ways to accomplish what matters most in your life.

Okay, so I've made the argument for not wasting time surfing the Internet if you want specific advice or answers tailored to your personal circumstances. But, how do you know what questions to ask or even where to start? Who can you trust to know and do what's best for you? These are all very important questions. The more knowledge you have of your financial situation and the options available to you, the more successful you will be. This is true even if you're a do-it-yourselfer or if you're working with a professional financial planner.

Information is not knowledge. Wisdom is knowledge and knowledge is power! A professional financial advisor serves a very important role in our society and possibly in your life. But, they shouldn't have all the power. Remember - no one will look after your money better than you will.

Arm yourself with the knowledge to ask the important questions, be able to make informed decisions and to select the most appropriate advisor for you... if and when you need one. This little book is a great start. It's concise, easy to read, and packed with the knowledge you need to best take advantage of the Social Security system. A Social Security Owner's Manual is the most refreshing, enjoyable, and directly applicable resource I've ever read on the subject. Invest the time to gain this essential knowledge. You and your retirement lifestyle will be glad you did!

Sheryl Garrett, CFP® , AIF®
Founder of the Garrett Planning Network

Award winning author/co-author of:
Garrett's Guide to Financial Planning (National Underwriter 2002, 2007)
Just Give Me the Answers (Dearborn Trade 2004)
Money without Matrimony (Dearborn Trade 2006)
Personal Finance Workbook For Dummies® (Wiley 2007, 2012)
A Family's Guide to the Military For Dummies® (Wiley 2008)
Investing in an Uncertain Economy For Dummies® (Wiley 2008)

Introduction

Social Security has become a significant part of many retirees' sustenance, ever since it was first introduced back in the 1930's. As the traditional pension plan goes the way of the buggy-whip and common investor behavior leads to poor results in savings plans (if there are any savings at all!), the Social Security benefit becomes more and more important.

Unfortunately, the way Social Security works is a mystery for most folks. There's really not much in the way of guidance for using the system, and relying solely on the phone representatives from the Social Security Administration is bound to lead you to a less-than-optimal result.

As with most financial activities, it pays to learn as much as you can about your options, possible strategies, and the pluses and minuses of various choices that you make. This book is an attempt at providing you with the groundwork to better understand the Social Security system so that you can at least be well-informed of your options as you approach the date when you begin taking benefits.

I hope that this book is useful as well as entertaining. I've done my best to ensure that the information contained herein is accurate and correct as of presstime – but laws change quickly, and limits are adjusted annually. Look for updates to this material at

www.SocialSecurityOwnersManual.com

How to use this book

It should be understood at the outset that this book deals primarily with Social Security retirement and survivor's benefits. Disability benefits are only briefly discussed.

In addition, while I've gone to great lengths to provide herein a comprehensive guide to the Social Security retirement benefits system, I've also been accused of providing instructions for building a clock when many folks only want to know what time it is.

With the many diverse sorts of readers there may be of this book, below is a guide to the parts of the book to help you navigate.

Part One is all about the inner workings of calculations used to determine benefit amounts. This section is good for financial advisors, attorneys, accountants, and others who would like a better understanding and a reference for how it all works.

Part Two explains the taxation methodology that is employed against Social Security benefits. Again, this may not be of interest to the casual reader.

Part Three details information about the Social Security Administration. If you are having difficulty with your benefit application, this section may help you. This section also explains the GPO and WEP provisions.

Part Four is where you'll find tips and strategies that you might use in developing your Social Security benefit plans. This section may be the most useful for the average reader, while the other sections provide supporting information.

Part Five is where I dust off the crystal ball and provide you with some guesses as to what may be coming for the future of Social Security. This one is probably the least useful as it's bound to be inaccurate five minutes after the book is printed, but it makes for a nice round number of "Parts".

Part 1: The Basics

The Basic Components

1. Eligibility

Let's start at the very beginning – it's a very good place to start. (Please don't break into song, people around you will wonder how you're getting so much fun out of a Social Security book. I'd hate to lose credibility with the first line.)

It's important at the outset to understand just how you can become eligible for Social Security benefits, so that you are clear on how eligibility works.

In order to be eligible to receive Social Security benefits - retirement, disability, or survivor benefits - a worker must earn eligibility to receive the benefits. The general rule of thumb is that for full benefits, the worker born in 1929 or later must earn at least 40 quarters of credit within the system.

Social Security Credit

A quarter of Social Security credit is earned for each $1,120 earned per calendar quarter (in 2011). This amount is indexed each year - for example, the amount of earnings for a credit in 2009 was $1,090. So if a worker earns at least $4,480 in 2011 (spread over the four quarters), four quarters of credit are earned with the Social Security system. The maximum number of credits that can be earned in any year is four.

Minimum Credits

The minimum number of quarters of credits for retirement benefits, as mentioned above, is 40 for anyone born in 1929 or later.

For disability benefits, if you become disabled before age 62, disability benefits may be available to you if you have at least six quarters of credits earned. Of course, these benefits may be reduced from the maximum, based upon your age and how many credits you happen to have earned.

If you've only earned the minimum 6 credits and you're under age 24, you are eligible for the full disability benefits. As your age increases, the minimum credits for full disability benefits increases to the maximum requirement of 40 credits by age 62 – ten years' worth. See Chapter 13 for a complete explanation.

Eligibility for Spousal Benefits

If you are married to someone who has filed for benefits, and you've been married to him or her for at least 12 months, your only qualification to receive Spousal Benefits is that you are at least age 62.

If you have been divorced for at least two years (and not remarried) and you were married to the eligible worker for at least ten years, you can be eligible for Spousal Benefits based upon your former spouse's record - as long as you remain unmarried. Your ex-spouse must be eligible for benefits (doesn't have to be taking them) and you must be at least age 62 for early benefits. The same rules apply as if you were still married, except that your ex-spouse doesn't have to apply for benefits in order for the divorced spouse to be eligible for the Spousal Benefit.

However - if you remarry at any time while your ex-spouse is still alive, you will become ineligible for the Spousal Benefit while you are married. If there is a subsequent second divorce or the second spouse dies, your eligibility is restored – to apply for Spousal Benefits on either ex-spouse's record, as long as you meet the criteria. If the first spouse (or any earlier spouse) dies, the widow(er) becomes eligible for a Survivor's Benefit as a Widow(er) (see remarriage rules for Widows in Chapter 33). You can choose any earlier spouse (if you were married more than once) for your Spousal and/or Survivor benefit - as long as you meet the eligibility (length of marriage) test with that former spouse. You can also switch to a different ex-spouse later if the other ex-spouse meets the requirements and would result in a larger benefit.

Note that I said "you can choose <u>any</u> earlier spouse" above, in reference to the situation where you may have been married more than once for the minimum 10 years. You are limited to only one former spouse's benefits. You could not collect two or more ex-spouses' benefits at once.

Eligibility for Children

If the worker is currently enrolled for benefits (again, they could have suspended[1] receiving benefits), a child age 18 or younger who is a dependent of the worker would be eligible to receive benefits based upon the worker's record.

---

[1] Suspending benefits is a tactic allowed at Full Retirement Age which provides a worker the option to establish a record with the SSA. This record allows dependent's and spouse benefits to be claimed on the worker's record, while allowing the worker to earn Delayed Retirement Credits. See Chapter 36 for more details.

2. Full Retirement Age

The Full Retirement Age, or FRA (gotta love the government for their acronyms!), is a key figure for the individual who is planning to receive Social Security retirement benefits. Back in the olden days, when Social Security was first dreamed up, FRA was always age 65.

Then, in 1983 the Social Security Act was amended to make changes to the FRA. Beginning with folks born in 1938, the FRA would be increased (see table below). For folks born in 1960 and beyond, FRA is age 67 (as of this writing) but don't expect this figure to remain constant. Increasing the FRA is one way to reduce the cost of the overall program, which is a constant concern for the government since this program amounts to more than half a trillion dollars in payout every year.

What's interesting is that, even though the FRA has been increasing, the "early" retirement and "late" retirement ages have remained the same, at 62 and 70, respectively. I suspect at some stage those ages may be adjusted as well, all in the name of fiscal responsibility.

The following table displays the current FRA ages by year of birth:

Full Retirement Age

Year of Birth	FRA
1943-1954	66
1955	66 and 2 months
1956	66 and 4 months
1957	66 and 6 months
1958	66 and 8 months
1959	66 and 10 months
1960 or later	67

Source: Social Security Administration

Note: persons born on January 1 of any year should refer to the FRA for the previous year.

3. Average Indexed Monthly Earnings

(AIME)

Another key component in determining your Social Security retirement benefit is called the Average Indexed Monthly Earnings, or AIME (there's another acronym - get used to it). The AIME is calculated by taking the 35 years of your working life while paying into Social Security with the highest earnings (adjusted for inflation), and then computing an average of those indexed amounts. This is done by adding up all of the indexed earnings amounts and dividing by 420.

Gobbledy-gook, right? Okay, here's another way to explain it: as you work in a Social Security insured job, your earnings are recorded each year. Each year the SSA applies an inflation factor to the year, based upon the Average Wage Index (AWI, more on this later). These indices for each year of your earnings are adjusted annually, reflecting the new AWI applied.

Once you are eligible for retirement (age 62, your Earliest Eligibility Age, or EEA), these years of earnings are put into a table and the indexes applied. Below is an example of an earnings table with indices applied:

Average Indexed Monthly Earnings

Age	Earnings	Index	Indexed Earnings
22	$ 5,000.00	7.4186559	$37,093.28
23	$ 5,589.41	7.0133446	$39,200.47
24	$ 5,771.91	6.6817598	$38,566.51
25	$ 5,951.90	6.362084	$37,866.51
26	$ 6,259.69	5.794243	$36,270.16
27	$ 6,598.18	5.453047	$35,980.19
28	$ 6,724.29	5.147081	$34,610.48
29	$ 7,263.44	4.789173	$34,785.89
30	$ 7,652.52	4.480037	$34,283.57
31	$ 8,151.79	4.226722	$34,455.35
32	$ 8,771.10	3.915769	$34,345.61
33	$ 9,095.79	3.600777	$32,751.90
34	$ 9,809.52	3.303241	$32,403.21
35	$10,300.66	3.001138	$30,913.71
36	$11,796.26	2.84454	$33,554.93
37	$12,072.71	2.712404	$32,746.07
38	$13,417.50	2.561809	$34,373.08
39	$15,014.39	2.457123	$36,892.20
40	$16,488.37	2.386295	$39,346.11
41	$17,578.53	2.243234	$39,432.76
42	$19,816.33	2.137938	$42,366.08
43	$20,064.41	2.056512	$41,262.70
44	$22,795.36	1.965713	$44,809.12
45	$25,440.98	1.895091	$48,212.98
46	$26,801.49	1.802233	$48,302.53
47	$27,536.23	1.786866	$49,203.55
48	$30,992.15	1.740161	$53,931.33
49	$34,893.01	1.673097	$58,379.40
50	$36,396.83	1.595089	$58,056.18
51	$36,936.43	1.507145	$55,668.58
52	$41,035.24	1.432187	$58,770.12
53	$42,533.74	1.356586	$57,700.69
54	$45,383.43	1.285498	$58,340.33
55	$50,034.62	1.255546	$62,820.74
56	$51,454.51	1.243079	$63,962.02
57	$55,140.29	1.213416	$66,908.14
58	$61,014.02	1.159513	$70,746.57
59	$64,329.16	1.118584	$71,957.57
60	$67,170.90	1.06943	$71,834.56
61	$73,383.51	1.023004	$75,071.63
62	$82,983.83	1	$82,983.83
Average of top 35 years			**$49,898.35**
Monthly Average			**$4,158.20**

Source: Social Security Administration

This table shows that the wages earned in each year you were working have been indexed to compare with the current year's earnings. Then the top 35 indexed earnings years are averaged. This figure is divided by 12 to come up with the Average Indexed Monthly Earnings - your very own AIME. (Pure Prairie League had a hit song about this, if you recall, in the 1970's.)

With this table in mind, you can see how the AIME could increase if you continue working past age 62 - those earnings will be added to the table, and if your indexed earnings in the current year are greater than one of your lower earning years, the average would increase.

If you continue to work and your earnings are not higher than the indexed earnings from past years, your AIME will not increase. However, even if you're not still working, it can be beneficial to delay receiving benefits after age 62 or FRA, as this will increase the size of your benefit. We'll cover this later in Chapter 34 - Delayed Benefits.

If you continue to work after FRA and receive benefits at the same time, if your average earnings continues to increase, so will your benefit.

As you might guess, this AIME isn't the amount of retirement benefit that you can expect: more factors need to be applied to come up with your Primary Insurance Amount (PIA), and then your actual retirement age is applied to the PIA to calculate your benefit amount. But we're getting ahead of ourselves here. Let's find out what makes up the PIA.

4. Primary Insurance Amount (PIA)

The Primary Insurance Amount (PIA) is the projected amount of Social Security retirement benefits that you will receive upon reaching Full Retirement Age - FRA, in Social Security Administration parlance.

The PIA is one of the factors used in determining the actual amount of your retirement benefit - the other factor being the date (or rather, your age) when you elect to begin receiving retirement benefits.

So, how is the PIA calculated?

In true government style, this calculation can be pretty convoluted. You start off with your Average Indexed Monthly Earnings (AIME - which we defined in Chapter 3). Then, hold onto your hat, because it gets hairy from here (this calculation uses 2011 figures):

- the first $749 of your AIME is multiplied by 90%
- the amount between $749 and $4,517 is multiplied by 32%
- any amount in excess of $4,517 is multiplied by 15%

Note: these are the figures for 2011. The figures used (referred to as "bend points") are based upon the year when the retiree is first eligible to claim benefits - at age 62. See Chapter5 for an explanation of Bend Points. For updated figures, go to www.SocialSecurityOwnersManual.com.

So let's work through a couple of examples:

Our first retiree is age 62 in 2011, and is hoping to begin taking Social Security benefits immediately upon eligibility - to get what's coming to her. Her AIME has been calculated as $6,500. Applying the formula, we get the following:

- first bend point: $674.10 ($749 * 90%)
- second bend point: $1,205.76 ($4,517 - $749 = $3,768 * 32%)
- excess: $297.45 ($6,500 - $4,517 = $1,983 * 15%)
- For a total PIA of: $2,177.20 ($674.10 + $1,205.76 + $297.45)

The second example retiree also is age 62 in 2011. His AIME has been calculated as $4,000. Applying the formula:

- first bend point: $674.10 (same as above)
- second bend point: $1,040.32 ($4,000 - $749 = $3,251 * 32%)
- excess: $0
- For a total PIA of: $1,714.40 ($674.10 + $1,040.32)

You should note that the PIA is always rounded down to the next multiple of $0.10 - otherwise in the second example the PIA would have been $1,714.42.

And that's just the start!

Once your PIA is calculated, it doesn't just sit there like the boring number that it appears to be. Each year, if you're still working, your PIA will adjust according to the additional earnings you've received. And even if you're not working, the PIA forms the basis of calculation of your actual benefit. Each year, an annual Cost of Living Adjustment is applied, as well as any additional (increased) earning years that may impact your AIME. The age that you begin taking the payment of retirement benefits is factored into the equation as well, which you'll see in Chapter 6 – Calculating Your Retirement Benefit.

5. Bend Points

Caution – if math and calculations aren't of a great deal of interest to you, the following section may make you drowsy. Please proceed with caution, and try not to operate heavy machinery while reading this chapter.

Bend points (mentioned in the preceding chapter Primary Insurance Amount) are the portions of your average income (Average Indexed Monthly Earnings - AIME) in specific dollar amounts that are indexed each year, based upon an obscure table called the Average Wage Index (AWI) Series. They're called bend points because they represent points on a graph of various levels of AIME with the points applied, resulting with the PIA (and the graph actually bends!).

If you're interested in how Bend Points are used, you can see Chapter 4 – Primary Insurance Amount, or PIA. In this chapter we'll go over how Bend Points are calculated each year. To understand this calculation, you need to go back to 1979, the year of the Three Mile Island disaster, the introduction of the compact disc, and the Iranian hostage crisis. According to the AWI Series, in 1979 the Social Security Administration placed the AWI figure for 1977 at $9,779.44 - AWI figures are always two years in arrears, so for example, the AWI figure used to determine the 2011 bend points is from 2009.

With the AWI figure for 1977, it was determined that the first bend point for 1979 would be set at $180, and the second bend point at $1,085. The reason behind the specific amounts is unclear, but it's safe to assume that they are part of an indexing formula set up when the bend point concept was created. At any rate, now that we know these two numbers, we can jump back to 2009's AWI Series figure, which is $40,711.61. It all becomes a matter of a formula now:

Current year's AWI Series divided by 1977's AWI figure, times the bend points for 1979 equals the current year bend points.

So here is the math for 2011's bend points:

- $40,711.61 / $9,779.44 = 4.1629
- 4.1629 * $180 = $749.32, which is rounded down to $749 - the first bend point
- 4.1629 * $1,085 = $4,516.74, rounded to $4,517 - the second bend point

And that's all there is to it.

Note: 2008 and 2009 were unusual years: these were the first two years since the bend points came into use, where the AWI figures actually reduced from the previous year, and this happened two years in a row.

As a result, the bend points actually reduced from 2009 to 2010 and again in 2011.

Why Bend Points?

We covered what bend points are and how they're applied, but we haven't discussed just why they exist at all. If you've been paying attention to all of the higher math going on earlier in this section, you probably have a clue about it.

Bend points were put into place in order to ensure that folks at the lower end of the earnings spectrum receive a larger percentage of replacement income from the Social Security system, and as lifetime income increases, a smaller and smaller percentage is replaced by retirement benefits.

The income below the first bend point is multiplied by 90%, ensuring a high percentage of the first income amount is preserved. The income above the first bend point but less than the second bend point is multiplied by 32%; the amount above the second bend point is multiplied by a mere 15%.

Bend Points

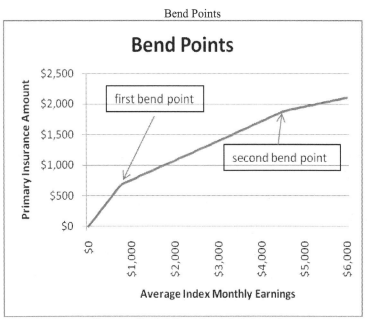

Source: Social Security Administration

As illustrated in the chart above, when your AIME increases, the corresponding PIA and ultimately your benefit amount decreases in the percentage of income "replacement".

Calculations

6. Calculating Your Retirement Benefit

There are three factors that go into determining the Social Security retirement benefit amount - your PIA (Primary Insurance Amount), your FRA (Full Retirement Age), and the age you are when you start receiving benefits. We covered the PIA and the FRA in the first section. Having these two numbers, we need to consider if you are applying for early benefits, and which would result in a reduced benefit amount, or if you're delaying receipt of benefits to increase the payment amount.

Applying Early for Reduced Benefit Amount

When you apply early (before your FRA), a formula goes into effect to determine how much your benefit will be reduced. First, determine how many months there are between your FRA and the age at which you'll start receiving benefits. The PIA will be reduced by a percentage based upon the number of months you come up with. The first 36 months are multiplied by 5/9 of 1%, and any months beyond 36 are multiplied by 5/12 of 1%.

So, if your FRA is age 66, and you intend to begin receiving benefits in the month that you are age 62 and 6 months, your PIA would be reduced by 20% for the first 36 months (36 * 5/9% = 20%) plus an additional 2½% for the remaining 6 months (6 * 5/12% = 2½%) for a total of 22½%.

> The maximum amount that the PIA can be reduced is 25% for folks with FRA of age 66, ranging up to 30% for those with FRA of age 67.

When you come up with the reduction factor, apply that factor to your PIA and the result is your anticipated benefit amount. You can see in the table below how waiting a few months or years can make a big difference to the benefit amount. This change can have a huge impact on your lifetime benefits - because once you start receiving your benefit, it won't change other than with the annual COLA increases - unless you continue to work while receiving benefits, which could increase your PIA. The other way to increase your benefit is to take the "do over" - described later in Chapter 30, although this method has been altered recently and has much less effect.

Delaying Receipt of Benefits to Increase the Amount

If you are delaying your retirement beyond FRA, you'll increase the amount of benefit that you are eligible to receive. Depending upon your year of birth, this amount will be between 7% and 8% per year (known as Delayed Retirement Credit or DRC) that you delay receiving benefits - which can be an increase of as much as 32½%. See the table below for the increase amounts per year based upon birth year:

Maximum Factors Based on Age

Birth Year	FRA	Delay Credit (DRC)	Maximum (age 70)
1940	65 & 6 mos	7%	131½%
1941	65 & 8 mos	7½%	132½%
1942	65 & 10 mos	7½%	131¼%
1943-1954	66	8%	132%
1955	66 & 2 mos	8%	130⅔%
1956	66 & 4 mos	8%	129⅓%
1957	66 & 6 mos	8%	128%
1958	66 & 8 mos	8%	126⅔%
1959	66 & 10 mos	8%	125⅓%
1960 & later	67	8%	124%

Source: Social Security Administration

So you can see the impact of delaying receipt of retirement benefits – you can receive more than a 50% higher benefit payment by delaying to age 70 versus starting benefits at age 62. Of course, by taking benefits later, you're foregoing receipt of several years of monthly benefit payments; if you start taking benefits at the earliest age, for several years you'd be ahead in terms of total benefit received. This advantage tends to go away as you age, though. The break-even point is reached in your early 80's in most cases, which we'll review a bit later.

7. Calculating the Spousal Benefit

The Spousal Benefit is one of the more confusing aspects of the Social Security retirement benefit system. It may be vaguely familiar to you that the spouse with the lower wage base is eligible for half of the higher wage base spouse's benefit, or something like that.

How is the Spousal Benefit actually calculated?

First of all, the Spousal Benefit is based upon a differential - between a percentage of the other spouse's Primary Insurance Amount (PIA) and his or her own PIA.

So how does this work? Let's look at an example:

A husband and wife are the same age with a Full Retirement Age (FRA) of 66. The wife has a substantially lower wage base than the husband. At age 62, she files for the reduced benefit based on her own record, from a PIA of $800. Her benefit is reduced to $600 due to filing early.

Later on, when they reach age 66, the husband files for benefits at his unreduced amount of $2,000 (equal to his PIA). The wife is now eligible for a Spousal Benefit, since her husband has filed. The benefit is based on the differential between 50% of his PIA ($1,000) and her PIA ($800). The differential between those two factors is $200 ($1,000 minus $800). This amount is then added to her reduced benefit for a total benefit of $800 (COLAs have been eliminated from this example to keep it simple).

Let's adjust the example: Instead of drawing her own benefit as early as possible, the wife has waited until FRA to begin drawing her own benefit, at the same time as the husband. Now her Spousal Benefit will still be $200 (the differential between 50% of his PIA and her PIA), making her total benefit $1,000 (her unreduced benefit of $800 plus the $200 Spousal Benefit differential).

What if the wife is younger? As long as she's at least age 62, she can begin receiving the Spousal Benefit as soon as her husband applies for benefits. It's important to know, though, that if she decides to file for the Spousal Benefit prior to her FRA, the Spousal Benefit factor is correspondingly reduced (as would be her own benefit if she filed early). Instead of 50% of her husband's PIA, at her age 62 the factor would be reduced to 35% of her husband's PIA, and then the differential calculated as explained before. This reduction is calculated as 25/36ths of one percent for each month before her FRA, up to 36 months, plus 5/12ths of one percent for each month more than 36 before FRA. The reduction factor is then taken against the original 50% factor to determine the actual percentage of the husband's PIA that will be received.

Reduction Factors for Spousal Benefits, FRA 66

Age wife files for Spousal Benefits	% of husband's PIA	Benefit if husband's PIA is $2,000
62	35.0%	$700
63	37.5%	$750
64	41.7%	$834
65	45.8%	$916

Source: Social Security Administration

Note: The roles could be reversed, with the husband taking the Spousal Benefit based upon his wife's record. Apologies for the gender specificity, it just becomes very clumsy to refer to the "lower earning spouse" and the "higher earning spouse".

And lastly, what if the wife has not filed for her own benefit? Again, as long as her husband has applied, she can file for the Spousal Benefit based upon his PIA. If she's at FRA there is no differential between her PIA (since she hasn't filed) and his factor-applied PIA, so the 50% factor is applied to his PIA and that will be her Spousal Benefit - until she files for her own benefit. When she files for her own benefit, the Spousal Benefit calculation will once again be based on the differential between the two PIA's.

If she hasn't filed and she's under FRA, her own benefit <u>will automatically be filed for</u> when she files for Spousal Benefits, under a rule known as "deemed filing". Since she's younger than FRA, when the deemed filing occurs, there will still be a differential between her PIA and her spouse's PIA, and that reduced Spousal Benefit differential would be added to her early-filing-reduced benefit to provide the total benefit.

It is important to note that if the spouse with the lower income files for retirement benefits before FRA and is <u>eligible at that time</u> for the Spousal Benefit (that is, the spouse with the higher income has also filed for benefits), then deemed filing takes effect and both the retirement benefit AND the spousal benefit will be permanently reduced. This applies ONLY if the lower income spouse is eligible for both benefits in the month that he or she first applies for a retirement benefit prior to FRA. See Chapter 37 for more details and examples of Deemed Filing.

See Part 4, especially Chapters 32 through 39, for additional information on Spousal Benefit tactics that you can consider.

8. Calculating the Survivor Benefit

The Social Security system has provisions for taking care of surviving spouses of workers who have earned credits under the system. There are two particular benefits that you should be aware of - a small lump-sum death benefit of $255, and a Survivor Benefit based upon the worker's Primary Insurance Amount. It is the latter of these benefits that requires considerable review.

The Social Security Survivor Benefit

When a primary wage earner dies, the Social Security system has a way to help care for the surviving spouse. The Survivor Benefit is generally equal to the primary wage earner's retirement benefit, and this benefit replaces any other spousal retirement benefits. You cannot receive a Survivor Benefit and a Spousal or regular retirement benefit at the same time.

The mechanics of the Social Security Survivor Benefit can apply to widows or widowers at various ages, depending upon the circumstances, as well as to the children and/or parents of the primary worker, if they are considered dependents of the primary worker. We'll cover each category in turn.

Widows and Widowers

When the primary wage earner dies, the surviving spouse is entitled to receive a survivor's benefit based on the primary wage earner's retirement benefit. Of course, if the surviving spouse is currently receiving a retirement benefit based upon his or her own record and that benefit is equal to or more than the deceased spouse's benefit, the surviving spouse will continue to receive his or her own retirement benefit.

If the surviving spouse elects to begin receiving survivor benefits before Full Retirement Age (FRA), the benefit is subject to actuarial reduction, just the same as retirement benefits are reduced. Since a surviving spouse is eligible to begin receiving early benefits at age 60 (instead of age 62 for regular or spousal benefits), the "usual" age table is shifted by 2 years. Whereas FRA for regular or spousal benefits for those born between 1943 and 1954 is age 66, for a survivor benefit, FRA for those born between 1945 and 1956 is age 66. (See Chapter 2 for the FRA ages and actuarial adjustments. Adjust the birth year by 2 for Survivor Benefit.) If the surviving spouse is disabled, early benefits may be received as early as age 50, with the actuarial reduction assuming benefits begin at age 60 (no further reduction, in other words).

In addition to the benefit mentioned above, there is a Survivor Benefit available to a surviving spouse who is not yet age 60 or older if there are children under age 16 that the surviving spouse is caring for, or a child of any age who has become disabled before age 22. This Survivor Benefit is equal to 75% of the FRA benefit of the deceased spouse - and only lasts until the child reaches age 16. At the same time, each child under age 18 will also receive a Survivor Benefit (more on this later) until age 18.

It should be noted that there is no increase in benefits by delaying receipt of benefits after FRA (same as the Spousal Benefit), so a widow or widower should begin taking Survivor Benefits no later than FRA.

It should also be noted that divorced spouses who survive a deceased worker are also eligible for the Survivor Benefit, as long as they were married for at least 10 years.

Children

Any child under age 18 (19 if attending school) who survives a deceased worker that has earned the maximum credits is eligible to receive a Survivor Benefit equal to 75% of the FRA benefit of the deceased parent.

If the child is disabled, the age limit does not apply – the disabled child of a deceased, eligible worker can continue to receive the Survivor Benefit for the remainder of his or her life. The disability must have begun prior to age 22.

In addition to the children of the deceased worker, this benefit can be available to step-children, grandchildren, step-grandchildren, or adopted children of the deceased worker, as long as the deceased worker provided 50% or more support to the child.

Surviving Parents Over Age 62

In the event that the deceased worker had provided more than 50% of the support of one or more older parents (over age 62), the surviving parents will also be eligible to receive a Survivor Benefit. This Survivor Benefit is based on the age of the surviving parent, and actuarial reductions apply to these benefits if received before FRA of the survivor.

Family Maximum

For the whole family of the deceased wage earner, that is, surviving children under 18, spouse and parents, there is a maximum benefit amount that applies - equal to between 150% and 180% of the deceased worker's basic benefit (specific calculations in Chapter 9).

Bear in mind that any Survivor Benefit received by a surviving divorced spouse does not count toward this family maximum.

9. Calculating the Family Maximum Benefit

When members of an eligible worker's family are receiving benefits based upon the worker's record, such as spousal benefits, benefits for children, or other family members benefits, there is a maximum amount of benefit that can be distributed in total. (There is a separate maximum benefit computation for disability benefits, which we'll cover in Chapter 15.)

How the Family Maximum Benefit is Computed

When computing the Family Maximum Benefit (FMB), the Social Security Administration falls back to its old habits of using a very convoluted formula, similar to the formula for computing the Primary Insurance Amount (PIA). The formula starts with the PIA, breaking it into four separate portions based upon Bend Points (and no, these are not the same Bend Points as those used in determining the retirement benefit).

> If you don't want to follow the math behind the calculation of the Bend Points, you can go ahead and skip down to the last paragraph - there we talk about the actual computation for the current year.

The Bend Points for FMB are based upon when they were first calculated in 1979. At that time, the Average Wage Index (AWI) was $9,779.44 for 1977 (remember, the AWI is always two years behind) - and for 2009 the AWI is $40,711.61. Dividing the 2009 AWI by the 1977 AWI gives us a factor of 4.1630.

The original Bend Points for FMB were: $230, $332, and $433. Multiplying these Bend Points by our factor of 4.1630 gives us FMB Bend Points of $957, $1,382, and $1,803 for 2011. These are rounded to the nearest dollar.

Computation for the Current Year

So here's how we use those bend points to determine the FMB, for a worker who becomes age 62 or dies in 2011 before attaining age 62:

1) 150% of the first $957 of the PIA, plus
2) 272% of the amount between $957 and $1,382 of the PIA, plus
3) 134% of the amount between $1,382 and $1,803 of the PIA, plus
4) 175% of the amount above $1,803 of the PIA.

The total of the four amounts is then rounded to the next lower multiple of $.10 if it's not already a multiple of $.10.

Family Maximum Benefit Bend Points

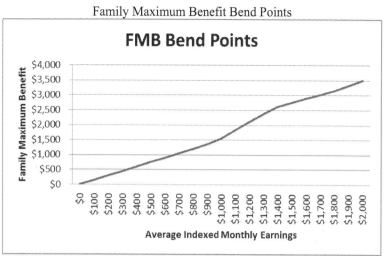

Source: Social Security Administration

Here's an example:

A worker age 62 with a PIA of $2,000 has a FMB calculated as follows:

1) 150% times $957 = $1,435.50
2) 272% times $425 ($1,382 minus $957) = $1,156.00
3) 134% times $421 ($1,803 minus $1,382) = $564.14
4) 175% times $197 ($2,000 minus $1,803) = $344.75

Adding these together ($1,435.50 + $1,156.00 + $564.14 + $344.75) equals $3,500.39, rounded down to a FMB of $3,500.30 for this particular worker in 2011.

10. The Impact of Zero Years

Remember when we talked about how your Social Security Benefit is calculated in chapter 6? Your highest (indexed) 35 earning years during your career are put into a formula, then averaged by dividing the result by 420, the number of months in 35 years. And if you have less than 35 years of earnings, any missing years become zeros.

So, you can guess what might happen when you have years with zero earnings in your record. Naturally your average is going to be reduced (possibly quite dramatically) by any year when you had zero earnings.

Let's say you have 35 years of earnings at the maximum amount, which will give you (for 2011) a FRA monthly benefit of $2,626. But if you only had 30 years at the maximum earnings amount and the remaining 5 years were zero earnings years, your benefit would be reduced to $2,531, an annual reduction of $1,140. Taking this further, if there were only 20 years of earnings, at the maximum amount, your FRA benefit would be reduced to $2,293, for an annual reduction of $3,996.

This often occurs when an individual chooses to retire early, or has years in which he or she has not earned during his or her career, such as when raising children or going to school.

11. Making Every Month Count

Earlier, we covered the benefit to you in delaying your Social Security application, but did you realize that even delaying a few months can have a significant impact on your benefit? This is the case for all benefits, whether taking them before FRA or after, since your age is always calculated by the month. Increase or reduction factors are applied for each month of delay or early application, respectively.

Early Application Factors

For each month prior to your Full Retirement Age (FRA), a reduction factor is applied. For the 36 months just prior to your FRA, your benefit is reduced by 5/9 of 1% - so applying a full 36 months prior to FRA will result in a reduction of 20% (5/9% * 36 = 20%). Any months added to that 36 will result in a 5/12 of 1% reduction, which means that applying an additional year earlier will result in 5% more reduction, added to the 20%.

So, for each month after age 62 that you delay applying for benefits, you'll increase the amount of your actual benefit - delaying to age 63 will eliminate 5% of the reduction versus applying at age 62. If your FRA is 66, delaying to age 64 will eliminate an additional 6.66% of reduction, as will delaying each additional year up to FRA. But the key is that even a few months' delay can increase your benefit. The amount of your benefit when you file is permanent, unless some other factor impacts it such as suspending or working while receiving benefits (more on these topics later).

Delayed Application Factors

When you delay applying for benefits past your FRA, you receive an increase in your benefit above your PIA. These increases are known as Delayed Retirement Credits, or DRCs. DRCs are (generally) better than the increase (or rather, lack of decrease) that you achieve by delaying application after age 62. For each month that you delay applying for benefits beyond FRA your benefit will increase by 2/3 of 1%, for a total increase each year of 8% (a little less for folks born prior to 1943).

So - make every month count! If you can delay even by a few months, it can make a long-lasting difference in your lifetime benefits - and potentially for your spouse as well, if he or she survives you.

It should be noted that DRCs only accrue up to age 70. At that point your increase factors have maximized, and no further factors will be applied. Of course, if you're still working and earning fat cash, your benefit could possibly continue to increase beyond your age 70, but that's a topic for another time. Suffice it to say that there is no additional DRC earned after you've reached age 70, so the latest age you should file for retirement benefits is age 70.

Disability Benefits

The foregoing sections (and the majority of this book) are focused primarily on Retirement Benefits. This section will point out some of the nuances for Disability Benefits.

12. Eligibility for Disability Benefits

As mentioned previously, there is a different set of rules for eligibility for Disability Benefits as opposed to Retirement Benefits. The minimum number of credits (quarters of work) is based upon your age, since it is very feasible that you could become disabled very early in your working career. The amount of benefits is correspondingly reduced to match the number of years you may have been employed and earning credits.

There are two tests that must be met in order to determine eligibility for Disability Benefits:

A "recent work" test, based upon your age at the time you became disabled; and
A "duration of work" test, to determine if, based upon your age, you have worked long enough under Social Security and have earned enough credits

If you become disabled before age 24, you need only 6 quarters (credits) during the three years before you become disabled in order to be eligible for disability benefits. And if you are between age 24 and 30 inclusive, you will need to have earned credits equal to half the time between age 21 and your current age in order to qualify. If you're age 31 or older, you generally need to have earned more than 20 credits for elibility.

The following table lists the recent work and duration of work credits required at various ages:

Recent Work and Duration of Work Credits

Disability at Age	Recent Work	During the Previous	Duration of Work
24 or younger	1½ years	3 years	1½
25	2	4	2
26	2½	5	2½
27	3	6	3
28	3½	7	3½
29	4	8	4
30	4 ½	9	4 ½
31 through 42	5	10	5
44	5	10	5½
46	5	10	6
48	5	10	6½
50	5	10	7
52	5	10	7½
54	5	10	8
56	5	10	8½
58	5	10	9
60	5	10	9½
62 or older	5	10	10

Source: Social Security Administration

To correctly use this table, consider if a person were to become disabled at age 44. This person would be eligible for Disability Benefits if he or she had worked a total of 5 out of the previous 10 years, and had earned 5½ years' worth of credits (22 credits). Likewise, if another individual became disabled at the age of 26, this person would become eligible for Disability Benefits if he or she has worked 2½ years out of the prior 5 years, and has earned 2½ years' worth of credits (10 credits).

You might be asking "How is it that the 44-year-old could work only 5 years out of the last 10 and still have 5½ years' worth of credits?" That's because the credits don't have to be within a specific number of recent years. The additional credits could have been earned more than 10 years ago.

13. When You've Stopped Working

When you leave full-time employment, there is a period of time after that when you will continue to be covered by Social Security for Disability Benefits.

Welcome to the 20/40 Rule.

The 20/40 Rule

If you have become disabled after you've left employment, you may be eligible for Disability Benefits - assuming that you're under Full Retirement Age (FRA). In a case such as this, if you have worked the required number of quarters to be eligible for Disability Benefits, the rule is that you must have worked 20 quarters out of the previous 40 quarters, earning at least the minimum.

The quarters don't need to be consecutive, but it must be 20 out of the 40 quarters prior to the onset of the disability. Another way to look at it is that for five years after you leave employment you will be covered by Social Security for Disability Benefits, again assuming that you're under FRA.

If you work, even part-time, ($1,120 earned in a quarter), this will count as a quarter for your coverage.

The 20/40 Rule is adjusted for age, as well. If you're under age 24 when you become disabled, you must have worked for 6 quarters out of the prior 12 quarters before you become disabled. Between ages 24 and 31, the numbers are half of the quarters after your age 21 - so if you're 29, you would need to have 16 of the 32 quarters after your age 21. After you reach age 31, the 20/40 Rule lives up to its name - 20 quarters out of the prior 40.

Once you reach FRA, Disability Benefits are converted to Retirement Benefits, so this rule doesn't need to be considered.

14. Disability Benefits at Retirement

What options do you have available to you when you've been receiving Social Security disability payments - and you're nearing Full Retirement Age (FRA)?

Disability Benefits at Retirement Age

As you reach FRA, your Social Security Disability Benefit will automatically convert over to a Retirement Benefit, at the same amount.

What does this mean? Essentially, once you reach FRA, since you're now on a Retirement Benefit, you have all of the features available to you as if you had not received any benefit prior to this point and you're now retired. So your spouse can collect Spousal Benefits based on your Primary Insurance Amount; Survivor Benefits are also available; and you can choose to Suspend your benefits at FRA (no need to File before suspending, you have effectively filed when your Disability Benefit converted to Retirement Benefits). (*More on the File and Suspend in Chapter 36.*)

By Suspending, you can earn Delayed Retirement Credits (DRCs) of roughly 8% per year up to age 70, which will permanently increase your own benefit and your spouse's potential future Survivor Benefit.

Obviously, there is no requirement for you to change anything at all once you reach FRA - you can continue receiving the Retirement Benefit the same as you have been receiving the Disability Benefit up to this point.

It's an unusual situation, understandably, but something to keep in mind if you happen to be facing this circumstance.

15. Family Maximum Benefit for Disability

Earlier we talked about the Social Security Family Maximum Benefit for a retired worker - and we mentioned that there was a separate calculation for the Social Security Family Maximum Benefit for a disabled worker.

This calculation is much simpler than the retired worker calculation for Family Maximum Benefits. Hang on to your hat, keep your arms and legs inside the car at all times, cuz this may get a little outtahand:

The family maximum for the spouse and children of a disabled worker is 85% of the worker's Average Indexed Monthly Earnings (AIME), but the family maximum can not be less than the worker's Primary Insurance Amount (PIA) nor more than 150% of the PIA.

Example

Let's use the AIME amount from the earlier example where we explained how it's calculated: $4,000. For this worker in 2011, the PIA would be $1,714.40.

So, the maximum family benefit for the disabled worker's family would be equal to the lesser of 85% of the AIME or 150% of the PIA, but not less than the PIA.

- 85% of the AIME: 85% times $4,000 = $3,400
- 150% of the PIA: 150% times $1,714.40 = $2,571.60

The maximum family benefit is the lesser of those two factors, or $2,571.60.

Part 2: Taxes

Taxation of your Social Security Benefits

16. Earnings Tests

As you know, you can receive Social Security retirement or survivor's benefits and continue working. If you happen to be less than Full Retirement Age (FRA) and you earn more than certain amounts though, your benefit will be reduced.

Note: these reductions are not really lost, your benefit will be increased at FRA to account for those benefits withheld due to earlier earnings. This later increase does not, however, apply to spousal benefits and survivors benefits that are reduced because of work. More on this a bit later.

Earnings Tests

If you're at or older than FRA when you begin receiving retirement or survivors benefits, you may earn as much as you like and your benefit will not be reduced. If, however, you are younger than FRA, your benefit will be reduced $1 for every $2 you earn over $14,160 before the year of FRA. The benefit will be reduced by $1 for every $3 you earn over $37,860 in the year of FRA, up until the month you reach FRA. (2011 figures)

For example, let's say your benefit is $700 per month ($8,400 for the year) and you are age 63. You work and earn $20,000 during the year, which is $5,840 more than the earnings test for your age. The Social Security Administration would withhold a total of $2,920 from your benefit ($1 for every $2 over the limit). This is done by withholding the benefit for five months, January through May - for a total of $3,500 being withheld. Beginning in June you'll receive your full $700 benefit, and in January of the following year you'll receive $580 extra for the additional amount that was withheld above the $2,920.

Now, if this year is the year you'll reach FRA - for example in June, and your earnings through May were $40,000 ($2,140 more than the limit), your $8,400 benefit would be reduced by $713, which is accomplished by withholding your first two checks of the year. The additional $687 will be paid to you in January of the next year.

17. The year you begin benefits

As we discussed above, there are limits to the amount that you can earn while receiving Social Security benefits.

What we haven't covered yet is just how these earnings impact your benefits in the year that you first begin receiving your Social Security benefits. Here's how it works:

Prior to starting your benefits, no matter when you start them prior to FRA, you can earn as much as you like. The earnings limits only apply AFTER you've begun receiving your benefits. In the case of the years prior to FRA, your benefit will be reduced when your monthly income is greater than $1,180 per month, for every month that you are receiving Social Security benefits. This is just a pro-rated application of the annual limit of $14,160 for 2011.

The same pro-rate method is applied for the year of FRA - the monthly limit is $3,155 for 2011.

18. Earnings Test is Specific to the

Individual

Another area that we haven't covered is the concept of your household income versus the individual. This is best explained by an example, which is illustrated below:

In this example, the wife is 62 and she works a part-time job earning around $23,000 per year. She is planning to retire in June, and so her total earnings for the year will be approximately $11,500. She would like to begin taking Social Security benefits right after her retirement.

The question is this: will her earnings test be based upon her "individual" earnings, or on the higher combined earnings of the couple (husband is still working, earning in excess of the earnings test amount)? Since her earnings of approximately $11,500 are under the $14,160 earnings limit, her benefit would not be reduced - but if the earnings test is based upon both the husband and wife's earnings combined, her benefit would definitely be reduced. How does this work?

Each person's earnings record is specific to that individual - the only time the spouse enters into the equation is in calculating spousal or survivor's benefits. Therefore, the only earnings considered for the "earnings test" for the wife in our example - are hers, and not the household (not including the husband's income, in other words).

Actually one other time that the household earnings are considered is when you file your tax return.

In addition, there is a special rule that applies to the first year of retirement, when a person retires mid-year: the retiree who retires in mid-year is eligible for a full benefit (however reduced by age, in our example wife's case since she filed before FRA) for any whole month that the person is considered retired, regardless of total yearly earnings.

"Considered retired" when at less than Full Retirement Age is defined as having earned $1,180 or less per month and not performing substantial services in self-employment.

"Substantial services in self-employment" is defined as more than 45 hours per month in a business or more than 15 hours to a business in a highly skilled occupation (e.g., brain surgery or writing a book about Social Security).

So, with this in mind, the wife would be eligible for her age-reduced benefit for the remainder of the year after her retirement, with no reductions due to earnings tests (as long as she doesn't pick up another job).

19. Payback When You've Earned Too Much

As explained in Chapter 16, when you've earned more than the limits, a portion of your benefit is withheld. However, there is an eventual "payback": when you reach FRA, your reduced benefit is recalculated, eliminating those months when your benefit was withheld, and likely boosting your benefit for the future.

There's a misconception that you actually receive back the dollars that were withheld due to your over-earning. That's not exactly how it works - you actually get credit back for the months when your benefit was withheld. This is much the same as how the "do-over" option works (details in Chapter 30), except that you're not paying it back to the SSA, they're just never giving it to you.

So, for example, let's say you took your benefit at age 62 (reducing the benefit to 75% of your PIA) and you had earnings that caused the SSA to withhold four months' worth of benefit each year for the four years between age 62 and 66. When you reach FRA you would actually improve your benefit by 7.22% - because your reduction would be adjusted to 82.22% of your PIA. The increase is because you did not receive benefits for 16 months during the period between age 62 and 66 (4 months each year when they withheld your benefit), which equates to a 7.22% increase in benefits when multiplied by the reduction factors explained earlier: 5/9% per month times 16 months equals 80/9% or 7.22%.

Part 3 - The Administration

20. Talking to the Social Security

Administration

I often recommend talking to the Social Security Administration (SSA), either at your local office or on their hotline, to review your particular situation. But this advice comes with a caveat: you need to know as much as you can about your options, and what you are entitled to do, so that you are well-armed when you speak with the SSA.

This is because the SSA representatives' default advice is often to recommend the option that provides you the largest benefit today. The reason for this may be because it is in the SSA's best interest for you to make your move now, rather than later. This is because up to age 70 any delay results in an increase in your lifetime benefit, provided that you live beyond age 80 (or so).

However, this also could be the case because a very high percentage of the eligible benefit recipients do not wish to delay receiving their benefit - so the folks you talk to at the SSA office are playing the averages by assuming that that's what you want to do.

It is for these reasons that it makes very good sense to know as much as possible about your situation and the options that you have available (and what you are entitled to) before you talk to the SSA. Explain to the representative what you're planning to do, and have the representative run the numbers to tell you what your benefits will be in the scenario(s) you're suggesting.

It pays to be informed - even more so when it's something as confusing and complicated (with so much potential gain and loss) as your Social Security benefits.

21. Checking Your Social Security Benefit

Historically, each of us used to receive an annual update of our benefit in the form of a statement. But beginning in 2012, this statement will no longer be mailed out automatically. But don't despair!

It's quite simple to check out your up-to-date benefit projection in the Social Security system - at least the retirement estimates. Simply go to the Social Security website (www.SocialSecurity.gov), and choose "Estimate Your Retirement Benefits" from the menu on the left. Next, choose the "Retirement Estimator" from the text on the page. You'll then be asked to fill in your information, including your Social Security number, birth date, place of birth (only the state) and mother's maiden name. Following the instructions, you will also be asked for the amount of covered compensation you received in the previous tax year.

At this point you will be presented with a web page that has your estimated benefits for early retirement (age 62), Full Retirement Age (depends on your date of birth), and at age 70.

22. Your Social Security Benefit Statement

Above we talked about how to get a Retirement Estimate from the Social Security. This used to be mailed to you just prior to your birthday each year, but is no longer being mailed. It's important to understand just what this statement (online or otherwise) is telling you.

Estimate

The page you receive when you fill in the form gives you the detail of your Estimated Benefits. <u>These estimates assume that your current earnings rates continue until the projected ages in the list</u>. First are your Retirement Benefits - at Full Retirement Age (your FRA will be listed), at age 70, and at your early retirement age of 62. These figures are especially helpful when planning retirement income, *assuming that you expect to continue earning at your current income level until the projected age(s)* and that you further expect that the Social Security system will continue to pay out to folks at your particular level of income in the future.

I'm a bit dismayed at the incompleteness of this new method of delivery (versus the old mailed statement), as the new method doesn't cover Disability Benefit or Family Maximum Benefit calculations. You have to calculate these factors on your own or seek them out elsewhere on the SSA website.

In addition, the Retirement Estimator doesn't list out your earnings record, as the old paper version did. At present there is no way of requesting this information online – presumably you can call the SSA or visit your local office to get this information.

I suggest that you do get this information from time to time to ensure that the records the SSA has for your past earnings is accurate and complete. This is the only way to find that information now.

23. How COLAs Are Calculated

As you are probably aware, each year your Social Security benefits can be increased by a factor that helps to keep up with the rate of inflation - so that your benefit's purchasing power doesn't decrease over time. These are called Cost Of Living Adjustments, COLAs for short. As of this writing, the most recent increase was for 2009, an increase of 5.8% - for 2010 and 2011 there was no COLA. But how are those adjustments to your benefits calculated?

Calculating the COLA

There is an index, compiled and managed by the Bureau of Labor Statistics, called the Consumer Price Index for Urban Wage Earners and Clerical Workers, or CPI-W. Changes to the index measure the fluctuations in those wages over time. Each December, SSA looks at the CPI-W level for the third quarter of that year (averaging July, August and September), and compares it to the same level for the previous year's third quarter. The percentage of increase, if any, is then used as COLA for Social Security benefits. This is an automatic process; no action is required by Congress to enact the increases over time.

As an example, the CPI-W average for the third quarter of 2009 was 211.001, and for the same period in 2008 the average was 215.495. Comparing the two amounts we see that there has actually been a decrease in the CPI-W. This is why there was no COLA for Social Security benefits in 2010. For 2011, it was more complicated. Even though the CPI-W showed an increase year-over-year, the increase was not more than the decrease that was experienced for 2009. Therefore, again in 2011 there was no COLA increase for Social Security benefits.

For the most recent example of an increase, the CPI-W for the third quarter of 2007 was approximately 203.681. When you compare that number to the 2008 third quarter figure (215.495), you come up with an increase of 5.8% - which is what the COLA was for 2009.

How it's applied

So, simple enough, right? We have the COLA, just multiply that by your benefit, right? Not so fast there, calculator-breath. Staying true to form, SSA has a more complicated method to determine what your benefit will be each year.

As we mentioned before in Chapter 6 on Calculating the Social Security Retirement Benefit, when you apply for benefits affects your benefit permanently. All benefit calculations begin with your Primary Insurance Amount (PIA), and are adjusted up or down depending on whether you applied for benefits after or before Full Retirement Age (FRA), correspondingly.

For example, if your Full Retirement Age is 66 and your PIA is $2,000, and you've filed for benefits at age 62, your actual benefit amount began at 75% of the PIA, or $1,500. The COLA is applied to your PIA, and then your reduction applied to that amount. So for a COLA of 3%, your new benefit amount would be $1,545 - calculated as PIA ($2,000) times COLA (3%) equals $2,060, times the reduction amount of 75%, for a total of $1,545.

Similarly, if you delayed your benefit to age 70, your benefit would begin at 132% of your PIA, or $2,640. For our example increase of 3%, your new benefit would be $2,719. Amounts are always rounded down to the next lower dollar.

24. Withholding for Your Social Security

Many folks find, upon filing their income tax return, that a portion of their Social Security benefits are taxable (often a significant portion, up to 85%). It's also often a surprise that, since the benefit is taxable, there hasn't been enough tax withheld from other sources throughout the year - which not only requires you to pay up come April 15, but it can also cause a penalty for underpayment of tax to be applied. This underpayment penalty is most likely if the amount of underpayment is $1,000 or more.

There are many ways to deal with this situation - it's not required that you withhold tax from each and every source of income. As long as you have enough tax withheld or timely estimated payments are made, it doesn't matter the source of the money paid in. Listed below are four withholding methods that you might use to help make sure you don't have an underpayment penalty.

Withholding Methods

Estimated Tax Payments. This method isn't actually withholding, but it achieves the same purpose. On April 15, June 15, September 15 and January 15, payments are made to the IRS. In addition, any overpayments that you made in the previous year can be applied in place of any portion of the estimated payments you've calculated. It's important that the estimated payments be made in relatively equal portions throughout the year, otherwise you may still be subject to an underpayment (or late payment) penalty. If your income from all of your sources varies through the year, your estimated payments should be in proportion with the income, net of deductions for the period.

Withholding From an IRA Distribution. This method is a little-known way to deal with meeting the withholding requirements. Essentially, when you take a distribution from your IRA (or Qualified Retirement Plan such as a 401(k) plan), you have the option to have the custodian withhold taxes and submit them to the IRS. No matter if you take a single distribution or quarterly or monthly distributions, the withholding is counted as evenly distributed throughout the year - taking timeliness of the distribution and withholding out of the picture.

Withholding From Your Other Income. You probably already know this, but you can have tax withheld from many other sources of income. Pensions, annuities, part-time work, and the like, can all be set up with tax being withheld throughout the year. This is accomplished by filling out a W-4 for a job, or W-4P for pensions - you can set the amount of withholding to literally any amount that makes sense for your situation.

Withholding From Your Social Security Benefit. Much the same as your other income, you can set up your Social Security payments to have tax withheld from each payment. This is accomplished by filling out a Form W-4V, and selecting the percentage of your monthly benefit that you'd like to have withheld - you can choose from 7%, 10%, 15% or 25% to be withheld. You can find Form W-4V at the IRS website or by calling 800-829-3676.

How much should you have withheld? Of course, that answer is going to be different for each person. It's determined by how much tax you are assessed, how much withholding you have from other sources, and the shortfall in withheld (or estimated payment) tax. If your withholding is such that your underpayment is greater than $1,000 you may be assessed a penalty for underpayment of tax.

GPO and WEP

25. Windfall Elimination Provision

If you have worked in a job where your pay was subject to Social Security tax withholding, and you have also worked in a job where Social Security tax has not been withheld, such as for a government agency or an employer in another country, the pension you receive from the non-Social Security taxed job(s) may cause a reduction in your Social Security benefits. This reduction is known as the Windfall Elimination Provision (WEP), enacted to eliminate the "windfall" that would otherwise be received by a worker who fits this description. Without the WEP, the worker would effectively be double-dipping by receiving full benefits from both plans.

This provision primarily affects Social Security benefits when you have earned a pension in any job where you did not pay Social Security tax and you also worked in other jobs long enough to qualify for Social Security benefits. However, federal service where Social Security taxes are withheld (Federal Employees' Retirement System) will not reduce your Social Security benefits. The WEP may apply if:

- you reached age 62 after 1984; or

- you became disabled after 1985; and
- you first became eligible for a monthly pension for work on which you did not pay Social Security taxes after 1985, even if you are still working.

Here's How It Works

True to form, the Social Security Administration doesn't make it easy to figure all this out.

You start out by understanding your Primary Insurance Amount (PIA), which begins with your Average Indexed Monthly Earnings (AIME), and then take the Bend Points for the current year into account. For 2011, the first Bend Point is $749 and the second Bend Point is $4,517. As we discussed in Chapter 4 on Primary Insurance Amount (PIA), the amount of your AIME that makes up the first Bend Point is multiplied by 90%; the amount from the first Bend Point to the second Bend Point is multiplied by 32%; and finally everything over the second Bend Point is multiplied by 15%. These three figures are added up to create your PIA.

However - if the WEP applies to your situation and you reached age 62 after 1989, the 90% factor (applied to the first Bend Point) can be reduced by to as little as 40%. Effectively, this reduces the PIA for those folks affected by WEP by as much as $374.50 per month (for 2011).

Exceptions

Again true to form, the SSA has exceptions to the rule. If it turns out that your service in the Social Security taxed job was for 30 years or more and you earned "substantial" wages (substantial is defined as $19,800 for 2011 and has been indexed over the years), then your 90% factor is not reduced at all. If you had substantial earnings for at least 21 years but less than 30 years, the 90% factor is reduced by 5% each year less than 30 years that you had "substantial" earnings in the Social Security-taxed job, with the lowest factor being 40%.

Additionally, the WEP doesn't apply to Survivor's benefits (but the Government Pension Offset does).

Other exceptions include the following:

- You are a federal worker first hired after December 31, 1983;
- You were employed on December 31, 1983 by a nonprofit organization that did not withhold Social Security taxes from your pay at first, but then began withholding Social Security taxes from your pay;
- Your only pension is based on railroad employment; or
- The only work you did for which you did not pay Social Security taxes was before 1957.

Limit on WEP Impact

There is a limit to the amount that your Social Security benefit can be reduced: no matter what your factor has been reduced to (from the original 90%), the resulting reduction cannot be more than 50% of your pension based on earnings after 1956 on which you did not pay Social Security taxes.

And lastly, the WEP also applies to Social Security Disability Benefits, using the same factors.

26. Government Pension Offset

There's a somewhat confusing situation that occurs when a spouse who is receiving either a Spousal benefit or a Survivor's benefit from Social Security while also receiving a pension from a federal, state, or local government. The Government Pension Offset (GPO) applies if the pension being received is from a job where Social Security taxes (Old Age, Survivor's and Disability Income, or OASDI) were not withheld.

What happens is that the Social Security Administration will reduce the Spousal or Survivor's benefit by a factor equal to two-thirds of the government pension that he or she is receiving. This is called the Government Pension Offset, or GPO. Those are the facts of the situation. Now let's look at "Why"?

Why?

Eligibility for Spousal or Survivor's benefits is based upon your own record with the Social Security administration. If your own benefit is greater than the Survivor's or Spousal benefit, of course you would not be receiving the Survivor's or Spousal benefit - you can only receive either your own benefit or the Survivor's or Spousal benefit, whichever is greater.

Since you are receiving a pension from a government job that did not require you to have Social Security tax withheld, your own Social Security record doesn't reflect the income earned from that job. The pension is designed to take the place of Social Security benefits - at least to some degree. This particular quandary was first addressed in 1977 with the amendments to the Social Security Act in that year - but it really went too far at that stage.

1977 Amendment

Government pensions from jobs not subject to Social Security tax withholding are designed to be partially pension, and partially compensation to replace Social Security benefits for the retiree. In 1977 an amendment was made to the Social Security Act to address the fact that, otherwise, a Spousal benefit or Survivor's benefit would be compensating the Spouse more than the system originally intended. The 1977 Amendment offset the Social Security Spousal or Survivor's benefit dollar-for-dollar for each dollar of pension received from government work that was not subject to Social Security tax (from a job that the Spouse or Survivor worked).

1983 Amendment

In the 1983 Amendment, the GPO was improved for Spousal and Survivor's benefits. Instead of the original dollar-for-dollar offset, now the Social Security Spousal or Survivor's benefit is only reduced by two-thirds of the government pension. This more accurately reflects the fact that the government pension is part pension and part compensation to replace the Social Security benefit.

When Does the GPO NOT Apply?

It's possible that your Spousal or Survivor's benefit may not be impacted by the Government Pension Offset. Listed below are several situations in which the GPO does not apply:

- If you are receiving a government pension that is not based on earnings;
- If you are a state or local employee whose government pension is based on a job where you were paying Social Security taxes
  - on the last day of your employment and your last day was prior to July 1, 2004; or
  - during the last five years of employment and your last day of employment was July 1, 2004 or later. Depending upon the circumstances, fewer than five years could be required for folks whose last day of employment falls between July 1, 2004 and March 1 2009 inclusive.
- If you are a federal employee, including a Civil Service Offset employee, who pays Social Security taxes on your earnings. (A Civil

Service Offset employee is a federal employee who was rehired after December 31, 1983, following a break in service of more than 365 days and had five years of prior civil service retirement system coverage);

- If you are a federal employee who elected to switch from the Civil Service Retirement System to the Federal Employees' Retirement System (FERS) on or before June 30, 1988. If you switched after that date, including during the open season from July 1, 1998 through December 31, 1998, you need five years under FERS to be exempt from the GPO;

- If you received or were eligible to receive a government pension before December 1982 and meet all the requirements for Social Security Spousal benefits or Survivor's benefits in effect in January 1977; or

- If you received or were eligible to receive a federal, state or local government pension before July 1, 1983, and were receiving at least one-half support from your spouse.

27. When GPO and WEP Apply

These two rules within the Social Security Administration's procedures reflect reductions to Social Security benefits for receiving pension benefits from a job where your salary is not subject to Social Security withholding. Usually these are federal, state, or local government jobs, including teaching jobs at public institutions. The WEP applies to your own Social Security benefit and pension, while the GPO applies to your spousal or survivor's Social Security benefit and your own pension.

The WEP may impact you if you are receiving a pension from a non-covered government job and you also are qualified to receive Social Security benefits based upon your own record. Survivor's benefits are NOT subject to the WEP. For 2011 the maximum WEP reduction is $374.50 per month, but it can be much less (even eliminated) depending on how long you worked in the Social Security-covered job and how much money you made there.

The GPO may impact you if you are receiving a pension from a government job and are qualified to receive Spousal or Survivor's benefits based upon your spouse's or ex-spouse's record. Your benefit may be reduced by an amount equal to two-thirds of the amount of your pension.

Part 4 - Tips and Strategies

28. Retiring Early

In earlier chapters, we discussed how beneficial it can be to delay receiving Social Security benefits as long as you can. If you'll recall, as long as you aren't in dire need of the money for living expenses, it makes good financial sense to delay receiving your benefit to age 70 in many cases, but of course not all.

The reason this is such a great benefit is that this government-backed income stream is pretty much as good as you can get, in terms of longevity insurance. When you start receiving the benefit, you'll continue to receive it throughout your entire life - at least under current law, and it's doubtful that politicians will have the stomach to change that fact. The reason that you should delay receiving your benefit as long as possible is due to the fact that <u>when</u> you start receiving your benefit impacts the amount that you will receive for your entire life - plus, depending upon the amount of your spouse's benefit, it could impact the amount that your spouse would receive as a Survivor's Benefit as well.

But there are times when it may make more sense to begin receiving your benefit earlier.

Starting Early

<u>Circumstances require it.</u> If you're in ill health, have a shortened life expectancy, or have very limited other resources, it may be necessary to start taking your Social Security benefit early. The financial calculations that we do to illustrate how delaying receipt of benefits is the better choice always assume that the recipient will live to at least age 80 or beyond, and can get along using other resources until age 70. If one or the other (or both) of these circumstances is not the case for you, it likely makes more sense to begin taking your benefit earlier.

<u>Spouse with a relatively small benefit.</u> If the spouse with the lower wage base has earned a relatively small benefit and intends to switch over to a Spousal Benefit as soon as it makes financial sense (may require a File and Suspend by the other spouse), it might make more sense to start taking the smaller benefit early, even though it is reduced. In this case the financial impact of starting to take the benefit early doesn't amount to a significant reduction in real dollars, so taking the benefit for several years is just extra "gravy on your french fries", in a manner of speaking.

Psychological impact. If you simply cannot stand the thought of leaving your Social Security benefit in the government's hands any longer than necessary - and you feel it's to your best interest to start early (even in the face of facts to the contrary), then by all means start early. If that's what it takes to ease your mind, you should do it - life's too short to be wrought up over such matters.

On the other hand, maybe Social Security doesn't matter to you. If you have more funds than you really need and the Social Security benefit is of very little real benefit to you - plus if you consider the Social Security system a "safety net" for needy folks, you might want to start much later.

As stated before, in most cases it makes good financial sense for the spouse with the higher earned benefit to delay benefits to age 70, but not in all cases. In order to really get a good handle on how these calculations would work for you, it may help to hire a professional advisor to run through the numbers with you.

29. Should I Use IRA Assets or Social

Security Benefits?

Folks who have retired or are preparing to retire before the Social Security Full Retirement Age (FRA) face a dilemma if they have IRA assets available. Specifically, is it better to take an income from the IRA account during the years prior to FRA (or as late as age 70) in order to receive a larger Social Security benefit; or should they preserve IRA assets by taking the reduced Social Security benefits at age 62?

At face value, given the nature of IRA assets, it seems like the best method would be to preserve the IRA's tax-deferral on those assets, even though it means that your Social Security benefit will be reduced.

If you look at the taxation of Social Security benefits though, you might discover that delaying receipt of your Social Security will provide a much more tax effective income later in life. In the tables below I'll work through the numbers to illustrate what I'm talking about.

Example

For our example, we have an individual who has a pre-tax income requirement of $75,000 per year. The individual has significant IRA assets available. If he takes Social Security at age 62, he will receive $22,500 per year. Delaying Social Security benefits to FRA would get him $30,000; waiting until age 70 would provide a benefit of $39,600 per year. In tables below we show what the tax impact would be for using Social Security at age 62, FRA, and age 70. In each case the required income is always $75,000. We also illustrate the individual living to at least age 90.

Taking Social Security benefit at age 62:

	IRA	SS	Tax
62	$ 52,500	$ 22,500	$ 9,556
63	$ 52,500	$ 22,500	$ 9,556
64	$ 52,500	$ 22,500	$ 9,556
65	$ 52,500	$ 22,500	$ 9,556
66	$ 52,500	$ 22,500	$ 9,556
...			
90	$ 52,500	$ 22,500	$ 9,556
Totals	$ 1,522,500	$ 652,500	$ 277,113

Taking Social Security benefit at age 66:

	IRA	SS	Tax
62	$ 75,000	$ 0	$ 11,113
63	$ 75,000	$ 0	$ 11,113
64	$ 75,000	$ 0	$ 11,113
65	$ 75,000	$ 0	$ 11,113
66	$ 45,000	$ 30,000	$ 7,953
...			
90	$ 45,000	$ 30,000	$ 7,953
Totals	$ 1,425,000	$ 750,000	$ 243,263

Taking Social Security benefit at age 70:

	IRA	SS	Tax
62	$ 75,000	$ 0	$ 11,113
63	$ 75,000	$ 0	$ 11,113
64	$ 75,000	$ 0	$ 11,113
65	$ 75,000	$ 0	$ 11,113
66	$ 75,000	$ 0	$ 11,113
67	$ 75,000	$ 0	$ 11,113
68	$ 75,000	$ 0	$ 11,113
69	$ 75,000	$ 0	$ 11,113
70	$ 35,400	$ 39,600	$ 5,901
...			
90	$ 35,400	$ 39,600	$ 5,901
Totals	$ 1,343,400	$ 831,600	$ 212,811

The difference that you see in the tables is due to the fact that Social Security benefits are at most taxed at an 85% rate. With that in mind, the larger the portion of your required income that you can have covered by Social Security, the better. At this income level, the rate is even less, only 85% of the amount above the $44,000 base (the provisional income plus half of the Social Security benefit). This results in almost $34,000 less in taxes paid over the 29-year period illustrated by delaying to age FRA, and nearly $65,000 less in taxes by delaying to age 70.

Note: at higher income levels, this differential will be less significant, but still results in a tax savings by delaying. It should also be noted that COLAs were not factored in, nor was inflation - these factors were eliminated to reduce complexity of the calculations. In addition, in calculating the tax, deductions and exemptions were not included. At lower income levels, where perhaps the Social Security benefit represents the lion's share of your income, it might make more sense to take the benefit earlier. Each option should be explored in full.

This is to assume that the individual has the available IRA assets to allow for the early use of the funds. Although in the end result, delaying to age 70 required less of a total outlay from the IRA, by nearly $180,000, in addition to the tax savings.

Hands down, this is a very significant reason to delay receiving Social Security benefits at least to FRA, and even more reason to delay to age 70. The only factor working against this strategy would be an early, untimely death, especially if the individual in question is not married. In that case the IRA assets would have been used up much more quickly than necessary, and no surviving spouse is available to carry on with the Social Security survivor benefit.

30. The Do-Over

The decision of when to begin taking your Social Security retirement benefit is very important. The problem is, we may not be in a position to delay receiving the benefit. Or maybe we didn't consider what a difference it would make to delay taking payment (it's substantial).

It's a little-known fact that you can re-set your Social Security payout amount during the first twelve months after initiating the benefit. You may have heard of this, but usually discussions have few details on how to do it. Plus, the rules changed recently, so you might need a refresher.

Let's say for example that you had a choice to begin your Social Security payout at your early retirement age of 62, at a reduced amount of $750 per month. Had you waited until "normal" retirement age (66), your benefit would have been 33% greater, or $1,000 per month. (For the purposes of simplicity of illustration, the annual cost-of-living increases have not been included in this example.)

Yes, these are real world numbers, and yes, the difference is that great. If you change your mind within the <u>first 12 months</u> of receiving your benefit, you have the option of paying back all that you've received to-date and waiting to apply later – with no consequence. The money that you received for the first (up to) 12 months could be a no-interest loan, if you wanted to work it that way. Of course the consequences of not getting this right could be very costly.

So how does it work? It's fairly simple - you pay back the Social Security Administration all of the money that has been paid out since you initiated the benefit. That's it, no interest, no penalties. Then you can re-apply for benefits at your current age or later, if you wish.

The only problem with this whole plan is this: you can only do this once, and it's not revokable. So, if you sent in your payback to the SSA yesterday and accidentally stepped in front of a bus today, your heirs do not get the money back. However, as is the case with each of these decisions, if you are the higher wage earner and your spouse survives you, he or she will be eligible to receive the increased amount as a Survivor Benefit.

Obviously this isn't a consideration for everyone, and it may not be an appropriate decision for many that do have the funds available to make such a move, but for some folks in specific situations it can be a pretty good move. As mentioned numerous times in this book, as long as you are in good health, the longer you work and wait to start taking the Social Security benefit, the better. This is especially true for the higher earning spouse.

31. History of the Do-Over

On December 8, 2010, the Social Security Administration published a revision to their "withdrawal policy".

What Changed?

Essentially SSA has decided that this rule, as it stood, represented a little too good of a deal, even though very few people ever took advantage of it. The original rule, in brief, allowed an individual to begin taking retirement benefits at any age above 62, and then at *any point* in the future the individual could pay back *all of the benefits* (without interest) and re-set his or her beginning date for receiving benefits. This strategy allowed the individual to receive benefits and invest them, then pay back the entire amount (but keep any interest earned or growth) and then receive a higher benefit due to the credits for delaying retirement.

Under the new rules, you can still use this strategy, but the payback is only allowed <u>within the first 12 months</u> of your receiving benefits. This doesn't mean that you have to re-set your benefit and continue receiving benefits at the 12 month or less stage - you could pay back your benefit at 12 months or less and withdraw from receiving benefits until much later if you wish.

So, the key here is that you couldn't, for example, begin receiving benefits at age 62, then at age 70 pay it all back and re-set. Those were the days, my friend. We thought they'd never end. But they did.

Under the revised rule, you're limited to only 12 months of received benefits before you pay it back. For example, you could receive benefits at age 62 until you've received 12 months' worth, then stop receiving benefits and pay back what you received. After that point you could delay reinstating your benefit until FRA or age 70 or whenever you like. Or, at age 63 you could pay it back and re-set to a benefit for your new attained age.

32. Spousal Benefits In Cases of Divorce

We've covered the spousal benefit for Social Security retirement benefits. It is also important to note that similar benefits are available to divorced spouses.

A divorced spouse is eligible for a Social Security spousal benefit based upon the PIA (Primary Insurance Amount) of his or her ex-spouse under the following conditions:

- he or she is at least 62 years of age;
- the couple was married for ten years or longer;
- he or she is not currently married; and
- he or she is not eligible for a benefit (on his or her own record or another ex-spouse's record) that would be greater than the benefit based on this particular ex-spouse's record.

The former spouse does not have to have applied for benefits, as long as the couple have been divorced for at least two years when he or she applies for the spousal benefit. However, the former spouse must be eligible for benefits - that is, he or she (the former spouse) must be at least age 62. Delaying application for spousal benefits beyond the former spouse's age 62, up to FRA (Full Retirement Age) for the former spouse, will increase the amount of the spousal benefit.

As with the regular spousal benefit, if the divorcee reaches FRA and is eligible for a benefit on his or her own record, the divorcee can choose to receive only the divorced spousal benefit now and delay receiving retirement benefits in order to build delayed credits, increasing the benefit available on his or her own account.

Any benefits that are received by the divorcee have no impact on benefits to be received by the former spouse, any other ex-spouses of the former spouse, or the former spouse's current spouse and dependents. The ex-spouse receiving benefits does not impact the Family Maximum Benefit (see Chapter 9 for more on the Family Maximum Benefit calculation).

33. Remarriage and Spousal Benefits

The Social Security Administration treats former spouses differently from widows and widowers with regard to benefits when the person in question remarries. This only affects ex-spouses when the other partner from the former marriage is still living. When the former spouse dies, the surviving spouse is treated as a widow or widower.

Remarriage Rules for Widows and Widowers

(For brevity I'm going to refer only to widows, but everything applies as well to widowers.)

If a widow is under age 60 and remarries (and stays married), she is no longer eligible for her Survivor Benefit based upon her late husband's record. After age 60, the widow can remarry and retain access to Survivor Benefits. This rule applies the same way for a widow who was divorced from the decedent, as long as she was married to the ex-spouse for at least 10 years.

Remarriage Rules for Ex-Spouses

If a couple was married for at least 10 years and has been divorced for at least 2 years, the ex-spouse can be eligible for Spousal Benefits based upon his or her former spouse's record - as long as he or she remains unmarried. Her or his ex-spouse must be eligible for benefits (doesn't have to be taking them) and she or he must be at least age 62 for early benefits. The same rules apply as if they were still married, except that the ex-spouse doesn't have to apply for her or him to be eligible for the Spousal Benefit.

However - if she or he marries at any time while the ex is still alive, she or he will be ineligible for the spousal benefit while married. If there is a subsequent second divorce or the second spouse dies, her or his eligibility is restored. If/When the first ex-spouse (or any eligible earlier ex-spouse) dies, she or he becomes eligible for a Survivor's Benefit as a Widow(er) (see above for remarriage rules for Widows). She or he can choose any ex-spouse (if he or she was married more than once) with the highest available benefit for his or her Spousal and/or Survivor benefit - as long as she or he met the eligibility (length of marriage) to that former spouse.

34. Delayed Benefits

It's usually best, for most things in the financial world, to act now rather than waiting 'til later. The notable exception is with regard to applying for Social Security benefits.

As you'll see from the table below, if you're in the group that was born after 1943 (that's you, Boomers!) you can increase the amount of your Social Security benefit by 8% for every year that you delay receiving benefits after your Full Retirement Age (FRA).

Delaying Receipt of Benefits to Increase the Amount

If you are delaying your retirement beyond FRA, you'll increase the amount of benefit that you are eligible to receive. Depending upon your year of birth, this amount will be between 7% and 8% per year that you delay receiving benefits - which can tally up to an increase of as much as 32½%. See the table below for the increase amounts per year based upon birth year:

Maximum Delay Credit Adjustments

Birth Year	FRA	Delay Credit	Maximum (age 70)
1940	65 & 6 mos	7%	131½%
1941	65 & 8 mos	7½%	132½%
1942	65 & 10 mos	7½%	131¼%
1943-1954	66	8%	132%
1955	66 & 2 mos	8%	130⅔%
1956	66 & 4 mos	8%	129⅓%
1957	66 & 6 mos	8%	128%
1958	66 & 8 mos	8%	126⅔%
1959	66 & 10 mos	8%	125⅓%
1960 & later	67	8%	124%

Source: Social Security Administration

So you can see the impact of delaying receipt of retirement benefits - it can amount to more than 50% of the PIA (Primary Insurance Amount), when you consider early benefits versus late benefits. Of course, by taking benefits later, you're foregoing receipt of some monthly benefit payments; given this, early in the game you'd be ahead in terms of total benefit received. This tends to go away as the break-even point is reached in your early-80's.

An Example

Here's an example of the benefit of delay in action:

You were born in 1946, and as such your FRA is age 66. According to the benefit statement you've received from Social Security, you are eligible for a monthly benefit payment of $2,000 when you reach your FRA (which would be in 2012). If you delayed applying for your benefit until the next year, your monthly benefit payment would be $2,160 per month - an increase of $1,920 per year. If you delayed until age 68 (two years after FRA), the monthly payment would be increased to $2,320, for an annual increase of $3,840. At age 69, delaying would increase your annual benefit by $5,760, and at age 70, your monthly payment would be $2,640, for an annual benefit of $31,680 - $7,680 more than at FRA. This amounts to a 32% increase in your benefit by delaying receipt of the benefit by 4 years!

Notes

It's important to note that this is not a compounding increase - that is, your potentially-increased benefit from one year is not multiplied by the increase for the following year. The factor for each year (or portion of a year) is simply added to the factor(s) from prior years. You also don't have to wait a full year to achieve some delayed retirement benefit - this delay is calculated on a monthly basis, so if you delayed by 6 months your increase would be 4% over the FRA amount.

The biggest advantage to delaying benefits is that you will not only increase the amount you will receive over your lifetime, but also the survivor benefit that your spouse will receive upon your passing. For some folks this can make a huge difference as they plan for the inevitable.

35. A Twist On Spousal Benefits

In this chapter, we'll be discussing an option that is available to all married recipients of Social Security retirement benefits - but you might not have thought of it. For most all married couples, it makes a good deal of sense for the spouse with the higher wage base - that is, the spouse that has earned the most money throughout his or her working career - to delay receiving Social Security retirement benefits as long as possible.

As described in Chapter 34 about credits for delaying Social Security benefits, each year that you delay receiving your Social Security retirement benefit past your full retirement age (FRA) can result in up to an 8% increase in your benefit amount. When delaying like this, it often also makes sense for the spouse with the lower wage base to begin receiving benefits at the lower rate, either at the early retirement age of 62, or upon reaching FRA. Then later, when the spouse with the higher wage base begins taking the increased, delayed, benefits, the spouse with the lower wage base will be eligible to receive the spousal benefit, based upon one-half of the higher wage base spouse's benefit.

But Wait, There's More!

What most folks don't realize is that, while the spouse with the lower wage base is receiving the reduced benefit, the spouse with the higher wage base can apply for a spousal benefit based upon one-half of the lower wage base spouse's benefit, beginning at the higher wage base spouse's reaching FRA.

While this doesn't necessarily amount to a very large payment, it is money that you are entitled to and should receive. The spouse with the higher wage base can receive this spousal benefit from FRA up to the time when election is made to begin receiving the delayed benefit based on his or her own record, at age 70. At that time, the spouse with the lower wage base will begin receiving the spousal benefit based upon the higher wage based spouse's benefit, as well.

Quick Example

Let's say Jane and Bob are a stereotypical couple - Jane didn't work outside the home while their children were in school, while Bob has worked and earned Social Security credits since age 21. As a result Jane's PIA is considerably lower than Bob's. (Keep in mind, the roles could easily be reversed, depending upon circumstances.)

So at age 62, Jane begins drawing her Social Security retirement benefit, in the amount of $750 per month (PIA of $1,000). They have decided to delay Bob's benefit as long as possible, to his age 70. Once Bob reaches FRA, when both of them are age 66, he can now begin drawing a spousal benefit based upon Jane's PIA. So Bob can draw a spousal benefit equal to 50% of Jane's PIA, or $500 per month.

When the couple reaches age 70, Bob applies for and begins receiving his full, delayed benefit - which is approximately $3,600 per month (PIA of ~$2,650). Jane's Spousal Benefit will be based upon the difference between her PIA and 50% of Bob's PIA - $1,325 minus $1,000 equals $325. This is added to her own benefit for a total of $1,075.

That's all there is to it. It may not seem like a lot of money, but why would you not go for it? The key here is that the spousal benefit that Bob can receive at this stage ($500) is greater than the spousal offset that Jane can receive ($325) since she's collecting her retirement benefit at the same time. So it makes fiscal sense for Bob to continue delaying receipt of benefits and apply for the Spousal Benefit at FRA.

It's important to note that this strategy and the typical File and Suspend strategy cannot be used at the same time. We'll talk about File and Suspend next.

36. File and Suspend

This is another provision of the Social Security system that is filed under the "Little Known Facts" section - although it is becoming more known these days. How it works and what's important about it is the subject of this chapter.

How File and Suspend Works and Why It's Important

Any worker can establish a benefit amount by applying at any time. But - after Full Retirement Age he or she doesn't have to continue receiving that benefit. The worker can immediately suspend the receipt of benefits, so that seemingly the application is unnecessary. However, what this has done is establish a "base" for the worker's spouse (and other dependents) to begin receiving benefits based upon that amount.

Here's an example:

A worker is at Full Retirement Age (FRA), and his or her spouse is the same age. The spouse of the worker has a much lower benefit available based on his or her own record, and is looking forward to utilizing the primary wage earner's earnings record to receive the Spousal Benefit.

At the same time, the couple prefers to delay receiving the primary wage earner's benefit as long as possible, to age 70, in order to receive the maximum increases. In order to achieve both goals, the primary wage earner applies for benefits at FRA, and then immediately suspends receiving the benefit. This establishes the amount that the lower-wage earning spouse can begin receiving in Spousal Benefits, while at the same time allowing the primary wage earning spouse's record to continue increasing in value until he or she reaches age 70, the maximum age to delay.

How To Do It

Because the mechanics of this option did not become available until 2000, believe it or not sometimes the Social Security Administration (SSA) personnel are not aware of this option. The application process for File & Suspend is not yet available online (as are most other benefit options) so you need to visit your local SSA office to complete the process.

In order to ensure that the SSA personnel are clear about what you're doing, you should download the Social Security Legislative Bulletin 106-20 (the link is at the end of this chapter) which explains the provision fully. The provision is part of the Senior Citizens' Freedom to Work Act of 2000 - and the third bullet point of the Bulletin is what you want to point out as proof that you can pull this number.

Soon enough, SSA personnel are going to get this one straight as more and more folks do this maneuver, so be patient with them, and print out the bulletin and take it with you to make sure you get what you're asking for. The bulletin can be found in Appendix A, and you can also find a printable copy of the bulletin at the following web address:

www.SocialSecurityOwnersManual.com/bulletin-106-20/

37. Deemed Filing

Earlier I mentioned how deemed filing impacts a person younger than FRA who is eligible for Spousal Benefits at the same time as he or she first files for retirement benefits. In a case like that, deemed filing rules requires that the Spousal Benefit is applied for at the same time as the retirement benefit for that individual.

There are a couple of circumstances that have to be in place for deemed filing to take effect. First of all, the spouse with the lower income must be at least 62 years of age, but less than Full Retirement Age. Secondly, the spouse with the higher income must have filed for his or her retirement benefit – either before or at the same time. The spouse with the higher income could have suspended receiving benefits after filing, the key is that he or she has filed, making the spouse with the lower income eligible for Spousal Benefits.

Often this deemed filing provision doesn't matter to a couple – if one spouse is filing for benefits early, adding the reduced spousal benefit is just extra gravy on top. However, it might be advantageous for the couple's overall financial picture to delay receiving the Spousal Benefit to FRA. It's possible to coordinate this, but you have to play your cards right.

The second requirement for deemed filing to take effect is that the spouse with the higher income has filed for benefits. If the spouse with the higher income has not filed for benefits on his or her own record at the point when the spouse with the lower income files, then deemed filing does not apply.

What this means is that if you can plan when each spouse is filing for benefits, you can effectively avoid the impact of deemed filing.

Here's an example: Phred and Ethyl, ages 65 and 61 respectively, hope to maximize their Social Security benefits. Phred, with a January birthdate, has earned the maximum wages over his lifetime, and Ethyl, with a February birthdate, has earned a much smaller benefit during her lifetime. To maximize their Social Security benefits over their lifetimes, the plan is for Ethyl to file for her own benefit as soon as she reaches age 62. Phred is going to delay his benefits to age 70 for the maximum benefit, both in his lifetime and in Ethyl's lifetime if she survives him.

Complicating matters, Phred and Ethyl are the legal guardians of their two grandsons, Chip and Ernie, ages 8 and 10. It is their desire to provide Chip and Ernie with dependent's benefits based upon Phred's earnings record.

The dependent's benefits could be provided based upon Phred's record now, if he were to file for his retirement benefit, but that would thwart the plan to maximize Phred's benefits by delaying to age 70. At some point after Phred's Full Retirement Age, he could file and suspend, thereby providing Chip and Ernie with the filed record in order to begin receiving dependent's benefits.

The problem is that if Phred files and suspends immediately upon reaching FRA (in January), he will make Ethyl eligible for Spousal Benefits when she plans to file for her own retirement benefit in February when she turns 62.

Let's tally this up: Phred wants to provide the dependent's benefits for Chip and Ernie based on his own record. At the same time Ethyl would like to receive her retirement benefit only (and not the Spousal Benefit), until she reaches FRA.

The way to accomplish this would be for Phred to delay his file and suspend action to at least one month after Ethyl files for her retirement benefit. This way, when Ethyl files, she would not be eligible for the Spousal Benefit (because Phred has not filed), and so deemed filing will not require her to take the Spousal Benefit. Then, at least a month later, Phred will file for his own retirement benefit and immediately suspend. This way the filing record has been established so that Chip and Ernie can begin receiving their dependent's benefits based on Phred's record.

If Phred filed at any time before Ethyl's filing (or in the same month), then deemed filing would take effect and she could no longer delay the receipt of her Spousal Benefit. Using the timing strategy detailed above will ensure that their plans can go as they expected.

38. Coordinating Spousal Benefits

You know from the preceding chapters that there are quite a few components to keep in mind as you and your spouse plan for your Social Security retirement benefits. It can be a challenge to work through all of them on your own. To help you with this process, I have listed below a guideline that you might find helpful as you plan. The point of this rule of thumb is to attain the highest benefit for the longest surviving spouse, while maximizing total lifetime benefits for both spouses.

The Spousal Coordination Rule of Thumb

First of all, we have to make some assumptions: we assume that the spouses are the same age (within a year); we're using the rate of inflation as the rate to discount future money to present value; we assume that any money received in Social Security benefits is offset by not taking that same amount from your savings; in order for the rule to work, your savings must earn at least 1% more than the rate of inflation; and lastly, we are not making a "guesstimate" of the date of death for either spouse.

So here's how it goes: if the lower Primary Insurance Amount (PIA) is greater than 1/3 of the higher PIA, then the lower earner should take benefits on his or her own record at age 62. Then the higher earner takes advantage of the Spousal Benefit upon reaching Full Retirement Age (FRA). Finally, the higher earner takes his or her own benefit at age 70, maximizing his or her lifetime benefit (and his or her spouse's Survivor Benefit). If appropriate, that is to say, if the amount of the lower earner's PIA is less than 50% of the higher earner's PIA upon filing for benefits at age 70, the lower earner should also take the Spousal Benefit at that time.

On the other hand, if the lower PIA is less than 1/3 of the higher PIA, once again the lower earner begins taking his or her own benefit at age 62, as soon as eligible. The higher earner files and suspends at FRA, providing a base for the lower earner to begin taking the Spousal Benefit at that time. And finally, the higher earner takes his or her own benefit at age 70, again maximizing the lifetime and Survivor's benefits.

I won't go into the details of all the specific calculations required for these two tactics to work their magic - because as with all rules of thumb there are bound to be specific differences in your own situation that will impact the outcome. Use these rules as a guide to help you think about the options, but put a pencil to the actual figures for your situation and make sure that they make sense for you.

39. Spousal Coordination Examples

There still may be some confusion about the best way to coordinate these benefits to the maximum potential. This chapter will follow a typical couple through the process using several scenarios, so that you can see the potential outcomes of various options.

Our Example Couple

Our couple for the purpose of these examples is named Lester and Selma, both age 60. The couple's future potential monthly benefits are reported as follows:

Spousal Coordination Surivor Benefit Example

Age	Lester	Selma
62	$1,687	$1,113
67	$2,469	$1,629
70	$3,090	$2,039

Note: These figures are made up out of thin air, and may or may not represent realistic figures. The figures merely give us an example to work with. We've also purposely set the couple to equal ages in order to simplify the calculations.

First Option: Both File Early (age 62)

Lester and Selma are bothered by the fact that they've had OASDI withholding from their paychecks over their entire working lives, so they decided that as soon as possible, they're going to start taking their hard-earned Social Security benefit. Let's look at the resulting amounts that this couple will receive over their lifetimes, assuming they both live to age 95:

Age	Lester	Selma	Total
95	$668,052	$440,748	$1,108,800

Seems like a pretty decent result, don't you think? But as we know, things don't always go the way we expect. Let's see what the outcome is if Lester were to die at age 72:

Age	Lester	Selma	Total
72	$202,440	$133,560	
95		$599,172	$801,612

The increased accumulated amount that Selma has received over her lifetime is due to the fact that she began receiving 100% of Lester's benefit as a surviving spousal benefit upon his death.

Now let's shake this up a bit and see what other outcomes we can see.

Option 2: Both File at FRA (age 67)

Having thought things over, Lester and Selma change their minds and decide to delay receiving their benefit until age 67, Full Retirement Age. Here's what happens if they both live to age 95:

	Start Age 67			Start Age 62		
Age	Lester	Selma	Total	Lester	Selma	Total
95	$829,584	$547,344	$1,376,928	$668,052	$440,748	$1,108,800

And again, since the likelihood of Selma's outliving Lester is significant, we look at the outcome if Lester passes away at age 72:

	Start Age 67			Start Age 62		
Age	Lester	Selma	Total	Lester	Selma	Total
72	$148,140	$97,740		$202,440	$133,560	
95		$779,184	$927,324		$599,172	$801,612

This is where it starts to get interesting. If you'll notice, under this option, when they both live to age 95, they are receiving a significant amount more by taking the Full Retirement Age amounts - a total of $1,376,961 versus $1,108,800 when filing early. This is a difference of $268,161 more.

Delaying start of benefits is also more advantageous when Lester predeceases Selma. When taking the early payment option, Selma would receive a total of $599,172 over her lifetime, while if they both delay receiving benefits to age 67, she'll receive $779,184, or $180,012 more in lifetime benefits. When you add in Lester's benefit over his lifetime to age 72, the Full Retirement Age option pays out $927,324 combined, versus $801,612 under the early option, for a difference of $125,712 more in total lifetime benefits for the couple.

So we have a rule of thumb that fits this couple's circumstances: It pays off in the long run to delay receiving benefits to a later age.

Option 3: Both File at Maximum (Age 70)

Very quickly, here are the results when both delay filing for retirement benefits to the maximum age of 70:

	Start Age 70			Start Age 67		
Age	Lester	Selma	Total	Lester	Selma	Total
95	$927,000	$611,700	$1,538,700	$829,584	$547,344	$1,376,928

And then here's the outcome if Lester dies at age 72:

	Start Age 70			Start Age 67		
Age	Lester	Selma	Total	Lester	Selma	Total
72	$74,160	$48,936		$148,140	$97,740	
95		$901,776	$975,936		$779,184	$927,324

As you probably expected, the total for both life outcomes is better yet with the option of waiting to age 70 to file. If both Lester and Selma live to age 95, they'll collect a total of $1,538,700 in benefits. The benefit is also greater if Lester dies at age 72, as illustrated above.

Our rule of thumb from above still holds true. But we've not necessarily learning anything else, beyond the fact that the rule of thumb becomes more true the more you delay - up to age 70 (no advantage to delaying beyond that age).

So, that's it, right? It's best to wait until age 70 to begin taking your Social Security retirement benefits - cut and dried. Hold on there, pardner! Let's have another look at the numbers, and the provisions of the system.

Option 4: Selma files early (age 62), Lester files at maximum (age 70)

Here are the outcomes:

Age	Lester @70	Selma @62	Total	Start Age 70		
				Lester	Selma	Total
95	$927,600	$440,748	$1,367,748	$927,000	$611,700	$1,538,700

And if Lester dies at age 72:

Age	Lester @70	Selma @62	Total	Start Age 70		
				Lester	Selma	Total
72	$74,160	$133,560		$74,160	$48,936	
95		$986,400	$1,060,560		$901,776	$975,936

This one takes a little bit longer to digest what happened. If you look at the totals, you'll quickly see that if Selma files at age 62 and both live to age 95, it's still better in the long run to delay receiving benefits for Selma. (For brevity, we've only included the Third Option to compare with, since it had the best outcome from the first three.)

But when you look at the possibility of Lester's dying at age 72, something different happens: the couple's lifetime benefits are greater if Selma starts taking her benefit early and Lester delays to age 70. This is due to the fact that Selma is receiving her benefit for 8 years (even though it's significantly reduced) earlier than the Option 3 choice - and then when Lester dies she begins taking her Surviving Spouse option at Lester's maximum amount. When you calculate the lifetime benefit received, Selma and Lester would receive significantly more - $84,624 in total - when Selma files at age 62, Lester at the maximum age of 70, if Lester dies at age 72.

This illustrates how Option 4 works out to a better conclusion if the higher wage earner dies early. This doesn't tell us a lot, and it doesn't conclusively give us another rule of thumb, so let's make another change.

Option 5: Same as Option 4, but Lester dies at age 80

So, is the outcome we found in Option 4 only good if Lester dies relatively early? What happens if he lives a while longer, say to age 80? Here's what happens:

Age	Lester @70	Selma @62	Total	Lester @70	Selma @70	Total
80	$370,800	$240,408		$370,800	$244,680	
95		$796,608	$1,167,408		$800,880	$1,171,680

Turns out that age 80 is the break-even point between these two strategies. If the higher-earning spouse (at these benefit levels) lives to this age or later, then the strategy of delaying both benefits to age 70 works out best.

So, for this couple, if the spouse with the higher benefit dies relatively soon after starting benefits, it makes sense for the lower-benefit spouse to file early. It doesn't need to be a focus, but the same would be true if the lower benefit spouse predeceases the other, higher benefit spouse.

How does this help? You aren't likely to know one another's expected longevity, and you really shouldn't plan to bump off your spouse just to make the numbers work out for you. You can take cues from your family history, present health, and the like, but in the end you just have to make a judgment call.

Some Final Notes

Bear in mind that the examples above are specific to this couple's circumstances only. Your mileage may vary – in fact your mileage will vary, unless you happen to have those exact same earnings levels (now that would be a coincidence!).

To keep from confusing matters too much, we didn't illustrate the spousal living benefit in these examples. What I mean by this is, as long as we've got one spouse receiving benefits and one spouse delaying to the maximum age, at FRA the spouse that's delaying can begin taking a spousal benefit equal to 50% of the other spouse's benefit. This would be more gravy on top of the benefits we illustrated above.

Also, in our examples we did not factor in Cost-of-Living-Adjustments - again, to keep things as simple to understand as possible.

There can be other alternatives to look at that are significant - especially if there is a significant difference in the ages of the two spouses. Maybe in an addendum to a future edition we'll look at the more complicated examples.

Part 5 - The Future of Social Security

40. Solvency

For most folks, the Social Security system and how it works is a mystery. Many believe that there is an account somewhere with your name on it, and you'll get to draw funds from that account when you retire. Other folks will tell you that the system is bankrupt or nearly so. Still others will swear that it's a Ponzi scheme.

These are mostly myths. So what is the truth?

<u>How The Social Security System Works</u>

In a way, the Social Security system actually *does* resemble a Ponzi scheme, in that the early participants paid in very little and received an inordinately large benefit (by comparison to what they paid in) – while later participants will be paying in a far larger amount, possibly more than they will ever get back out in benefits. To be a true Ponzi scheme though, the later participants would be told that they can expect the same return on investment that the earlier folks received. I think we've understood for quite some time that this isn't an investment, but a tax – and that ultimately we may get very little out of the system compared to what we put in it.

From the beginning, the Social Security system has overtly been a "pay as you go" system, meaning that current receipts from tax withholding are used to pay benefits to current recipients. Most of the time during its 75-year existence, the system has been paying out less in benefits than it was taking in from withholding, and so the surplus has been placed in a trust fund[2] to help pay for benefits in the future. This trust fund amounts to roughly $2.5 trillion these days.

This design was based upon the (incorrect) assumption that each succeeding generation would be larger than the previous generation, therefore the receipts would always be greater than the payouts. That was before the Baby Boom.

It has been projected that, beginning in 2017 (although I've seen it reprojected to 2016 lately) that the system will begin drawing from the trust fund regularly, although the interest alone on the trust fund's account will be enough to cover the excess needs of the system through 2027. At that point, it is

---

[2] Much has been said and written about the "trust fund". It should be understood that there is no such account with the $2.5 trillion in the balance. Congress has long since raided the trust fund and presently has a huge I.O.U. in the account. It's not clear how this I.O.U. will ever be paid off – stay tuned for more as we get to the days when trust fund monies will be needed to pay current benefits.

projected that the principal in the trust fund will be accessed to pay benefits, and the trust fund principal is expected to be exhausted by 2041.

So – What's Going to Happen?

I can't tell the future, but I have a couple of guesses as to what may occur. But first, I wanted to point out a couple of recent developments:

1) In 2010, due in part to the economic downturn, the Social Security system paid out more than it took in. This was not a catastrophe, and it is not expected to be a long-term trend, nor is it the first time this has happened. It was, however, unexpected, and may have a big impact on the crossover point projected in ~~2017~~ 2016. This is primarily due to unemployment staying high (less money coming in due to smaller payrolls). Stay tuned, but also see # 2.

2) The long-term trend that will likely have the greatest impact on the health of the Social Security system is the delay of retirement among many Americans, specifically the troublesome Baby Boom generation. According to some recent data, the percentage of folks between 65 and 75 that are still active in the workforce was 25% in 2010, versus 17% in 1990. That's a significant fact, because those folks are continuing to pay into the system, and either delaying receipt of benefits or receiving a smaller

benefit (at least until Full Retirement Age) than was projected.

The combination of these two factors is likely to improve the outlook for the overall system, although we'll have to wait for the ~~witch doctors~~ actuaries to sift through the numbers to know what the new projections will look like.

My Guesses

In the meantime, here's my guesses as to what may happen:

- Like anyone with a finite budget, when it comes time to begin paying out of principal, I expect for benefits to be reduced across the board – possibly by as much as 25%.
- But before that happens, I expect that we'll see increases to the ages for benefits, such as bumping up the early retirement age from 62 to 64, and the maximum benefit age from 70 to 72. These increases would match the increase in the Full Retirement Age that has been in place for some time now.
- Expect some sort of means testing to begin – meaning that if you have other sources of income (IRA, pension, 401(k), etc.) then your Social Security benefit will likely be reduced and possibly eliminated.

- And lastly, plan on the fact that pretty much any benefit you receive will be taxed to some degree.

Regardless, all this talk about Social Security going bankrupt is pretty much ill-founded. Since the system has the ability to draw in tax rolls it cannot be bankrupted; benefits can reduce and ages for benefits can increase, but it can't go completely broke. It's bad, but not catastrophic. It's sort of like if we were to discover that, after all of the sightings and legends over the years, it turns out that Bigfoot isn't really an unknown species, but rather that it was just members of The Allman Brothers Band wandering about in the wilds. Frightening, but not the end of the world.

So What Can You Do?

Write your congressmen & women. Light a candle. Wring your hands, and say "oh my". And in the end you may just have to learn to get over it, and realize that Social Security should not be counted upon as a significant portion of your retirement income – especially if you were born after about 1955. Concentrate on your savings, and then, if the Social Security fairy happens to leave something under your pillow when you retire, consider it gravy.

41. Methods of Calculation of COLAs

One of the many proposed changes that is being considered to help resolve the current budgetary issues is to change the index used to adjust Social Security benefits from the current method, using the Consumer Price Index for Urban Wage Earners and Clerical Workers, or CPI-W, to a much more conservative index known as the Chained Consumer Price Index for all Urban Consumers (or C-CPI-U). (See Chapter 23 on How Social Security COLAs are Calculated for more information.)

Unfortunately, the reason behind making this is change is the fact that it will ultimately save money for the Social Security system, directly at the expense of the beneficiaries of that system. Here's what you can expect:

As an example, the CPI-W indicates a year-over-year increase from June 2010 to June 2011 of 4.1%. Over the same period, the C-CPI-U only shows an increase of 3.4%.

This is due to the factors used in calculating the C-CPI-U, which considers that as inflation increases, spending on certain items will decrease, since consumers will purchase cheaper items or less quantity of items as the prices increase. The Bureau of Labor

Statistics, who tracks these things and comes up with the indexes, suggests that the chained index more accurately reflects the way real-live consumers operate with regard to inflation.

Estimates by the actuaries for the SSA indicate that this change could result in a $1,000 per year reduction of benefits (or actually, forgone benefit) by the age of 85. The estimate is that over any 30-year span, using the C-CPI-U instead of the CPI-W would result in a 10% lower total benefit being paid out.

Each year's increase, if this new index is put into place, is anticipated to be two- to three-tenths of a percent lower than the increase would have been under the current index.

The change in index is not only proposed for Social Security benefits but also for certain tax provisions as well, such as standard deduction, and tax rate tables. In both cases, the taxpayer (at all levels, not just the "rich") will be impacted negatively.

As always, the only way to try to impact this is to contact your representatives in Congress and let them know that you're not in favor of having your miniscule increases reduced further in the name of budget cutting. There are plenty of places where pork can be removed from the budget before hitting our seniors with this, in my opinion.

Index

Acronyms

AIME – Average Indexed Monthly Earnings
AWI – Average Wage Index
COLA – Cost of Living Adjustment
C-CPI-U – Chained Consumer Price Index for all Urban Consumers
CPI-W – Consumer Price Index for Urban Wage Earners and Clerical Workers
DRC – Delayed Retirement Credits
EEA – Earliest Eligibility Age
F&S – File and Suspend
FMB – Family Maximum Benefit
FRA – Full Retirement Age
GPO – Government Pension Offset
HES – Higher Earning Spouse
LES – Lower Earning Spouse
NH – NumberHolder
PIA – Primary Insurance Amount
SSA – Social Security Administration
SSI – Supplemental Security Income
WEP – Windfall Elimination Provision

Appendix A

Social Security Legislative Bulletin 106-20
See the following web address for a downloadable copy:
www.socialsecurityownersmanual.com/legislative-bulletin-106-20/

106-20

April 7, 2000

The President Signs the "Senior Citizens' Freedom to Work Act of 2000"

Today, President Clinton signed into law P.L. 106-182, the Senior Citizens' Freedom To Work Act of 2000.

As yet, a public law number has not been assigned.

The legislation:

- Eliminates the Social Security retirement earnings test in and after the month in which a person attains full retirement age--currently age 65. Elimination of the retirement test would be effective with respect to taxable years ending after December 31, 1999.
- In the calendar year the beneficiary attains the full retirement age, permanently applies the earnings limit for those at the full retirement age through age 69 ($17,000 in 2000, $25,000 in 2001 and $30,000 in 2002) and the corresponding reduction rate ($1 for $3 offset) to all months prior to attainment of the full retirement age. (In applying the earnings test for this calendar year, only earnings before the month of attainment of full retirement age are considered.)
- Permits, beginning with the month in which the beneficiary reaches full retirement age and ending with the month prior to attainment of age 70, the

retired worker to earn a delayed retirement credit for any month for which the retired worker requests that benefits not be paid even though he/she is already on the benefit rolls. On March 1, 2000, the House approved an earlier version of H.R. 5. The Senate approved an amended version of the legislation on March 22, 2000. The House agreed to the Senate amendment to the legislation and cleared the measure for transmission to the President on March 28, 2000. For additional detail, see Legislative Bulletins **106-16, 106-17, 106-18 and 106-19.**

Made in the USA
Charleston, SC
18 May 2012